SPECIAL EFFECTS

SPECIAL EFFECTS

IN FILM AND TELEVISION

WRITTEN BY
JAKE HAMILTON

LONDON • NEW YORK
STUTTGART • MOSCOW • SYDNEY

A DORLING KINDERSLEY BOOK

Project Editor MIRANDA SMITH

Art Editor KATI POYNOR

Designer IAIN MORRIS

Senior Managing Editor GILLIAN DENTON

Senior Managing Art Editor JULIA HARRIS

Production CHARLOTTE TRAILL

Picture Research JAMES CLARKE, SEAN HUNTER

DTP Designer NICKY STUDDART

Photography GEOFF BRIGHTLING, ANDY CRAWFORD

This book would not have been possible without the
contibution of: Nick Bolton of OXFORD METRICS; Pauline
Cox; Steve Crawley; Gordon Coxon and Richard van den
Bergh of EVOLUTION FX; Neill Gorton of GORTON AND PAINTER;
JIM HENSON'S CREATURE SHOP; Anthony Hunt of THE MAGIC
CAMERA COMPANY, Shepperton; Sean McCabe; Jason Parrott
of 4:2:2 Videographics; and Mike Valentine

First published in Great Britain in 1998
by Dorling Kindersley Limited
9 Henrietta Street, London WC2E 8PS

A CIP catalogue record for this book is available from the
British Library.
ISBN 0 7513 5359 0
Colour reproduced by Colourscan, Singapore
Printed in Italy by Montadori

CONTENTS

HAVING AN EFFECT

Special effects (SFX) is the art of making the impossible into a fantastic reality, and it is a thrilling element of film and television. Since Georges Méliès first impressed an audience with cinematic special effects in 1902, audiences have experienced a dizzying journey of nearly one hundred years of SFX breakthroughs. From camera trickery, animatronics, and prosthetic make-up through to blue-screening, and advanced digital technology, the history of special effects has always pushed the boundaries of human imagination, and keeps today's audiences glued to their seats in starry-eyed wonder.

Actors run for cover from imaginary alien ships during separate shoot

Computer generated imagery (CGi) created the battalion of alien airships

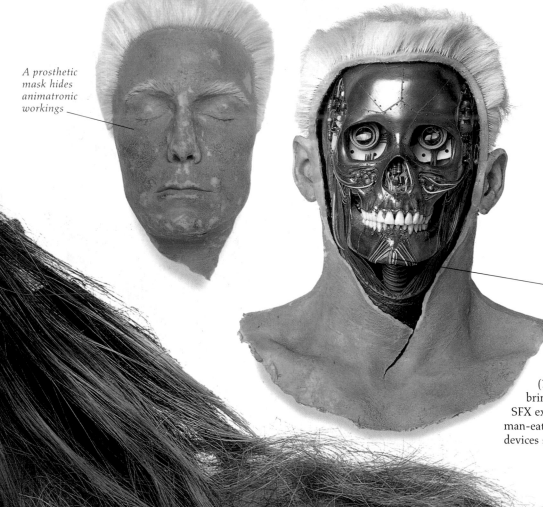

A prosthetic mask hides animatronic workings

The animatronic face can grin and roll its eyes

A human hand is transformed into the hairy paw of a werewolf thanks to the magic of make-up

DIGITAL MAYHEM

The extraordinary alien strike on US troops in the film *Independence Day* (1996) is a showcase of the amazing complexity in modern filmmaking made possible by special effects. Director Roland Emmerich first shot live action footage of actors running for cover from imaginary alien spaceships in the vast Utah desert. Explosive charges were set by pyrotechnicians, and the spaceships were miniature models digitally enhanced in post production. Effects animation was added to show the alien lasers zapping the US air base.

ANIMATED WONDERS

The use of puppetry and animatronics have created some of the most imaginative images in cinema from the ape in *King Kong* (1933) to the gorilla in *Buddy* (1998). Animatronics is the art of bringing creatures to life by means of electronics and remote control. SFX experts can now create mechanical human beings, talking dogs, and man-eating dinosaurs by the use of a wide range of puppet and animatronic devices such as motion rods, wires, electric motors and air pumps.

BEASTLY DELIGHTS

Make-up is not always reserved for the beautiful and glamorous. Sometimes special make-ups are needed to create hideous monsters and bloodthirsty werewolves. Fake hair, pointed talons and fanged teeth are often used in cinema to give horror films that extra bite! Actors often have to spend up to five or six hours in the make-up chair while a special effects team transforms their features with latex masks, deep scars, and coloured contact lenses (pp. 32–37).

Pyrotechnic staff planted remote controlled explosives around the air base

Effects animation was added in post production to show lasers hitting the ground

Tom Cruise gets soaked during a set-up rain storm in Mission Impossible (1996)

HEAVY WEATHER

Special effects are not always only involved in science fiction, horror, or fantasy. Sometimes, a SFX team are called on to create subtle effects such as a downpour of rain, a wind storm, or a blinding ray of sun. Film crews often use huge wind machines, high-powered fans, and rain cranes to give dramatic scenes that extra edge. Fake snow is also used, and SFX technicians can create dramatic tornadoes or volcanoes with computer generated images.

A strange alien rib cage has been created with foam latex and special paints

The actor's hands are disguised as elongated alien claws

PROSTHETIC MONSTERS

The human face and body can be radically transformed thanks to the process of prosthetics, a special effects term used for make-up which can create a whole new skin and bone structure built around a particular actor or actress. Using form-changing materials such as foam latex, gelatine, and plaster, the make-up expert can create terrifying aliens with huge jaws, or simply alter an actor's eyebrow slightly to good effect.

This whole body prosthetic comes complete with fangs

The model-maker has built huge muscles to underline the creature's great strength

TELLING A STORY

When a movie is being planned, a storyboard is is prepared for every scene. Storyboards are pictures, often in a sequence, of what will be seen in each part of a film, shot by shot. They may be just a few basic outline sketches showing a scene, or single, huge drawings of alien creatures. The pictures act as a guide to the director and the other people working on a movie such as the costume designer, model-makers, pyrotechnicians, and camera operators, so that the whole crew is working towards achieving the same result. For every action sequence, there is a storyboard prepared so that the special effects team can plan in detail all the effects needed. Underneath each drawing, there will be a description of the action, some technical details on where the camera will be placed, and perhaps some of the actors' dialogue.

CHARACTER PLANNING
Aliens and animals are given character storyboards just like any other actor in a film. These creatures have to be developed from scratch and the director must know what they look like, how tall they are, and how they move about before any filming begins. This storyboard for the extra-terrestrial in *E.T.* (1982) shows the head and body parts of the alien, and was used to discuss how it makes facial expressions.

SETTING OUT A STORYBOARD
Every special effects sequence is created on paper first. Detailed drawings are made and studied to check that the sequences can be achieved. This storyboard from *The Borrowers* (1997) shows, step by step, a particular sequence set in a bottle factory. There are labelled sketches, technical notes, and directions for shots.

Dialogue and technical notes are jotted underneath for every shot

Special effects sequence drawings involving two Borrower children

SET DECORATION
Before any scenes are filmed or actors chosen for key roles, film producers must decide what the film will look like, and what kind of atmosphere is needed. This work is done by a set decorator who will sketch out storyboards for strange buildings and beautiful landscapes. For the puppet film *Dark Crystal* (1983), an elaborate fantasy world where good and evil battle to save the planet was created.

COSTUME PLANNING
Costume design sometimes needs the help of the special effects team. For *The Borrowers*, costume designers had taken into account that the tiny Clock family who live under the floorboards would make their clothes from bits and pieces of giant human people's clothing. Arriety Clock (above) had a shirt made from a shirt cuff with a lifesize button and paper clip attached.

GOING, GOING, GONE

The original storyboard for the burning of the city of Atlanta in *Gone With the Wind* (1939) was so accurate and detailed that producers shot the scene exactly how it looked on the page. More than 1.2 hectares (30 acres) of the old Pathé studio backlot in Hollywood was put to the torch, including the set built for the film *King Kong* (1933). Seven Technicolor cameras recorded the whole dramatic sequence referring to directions given on the storyboard.

The still from the film is remarkably like the storyboard drawing

Detailed drawings show Rhett Butler and Scarlett O'Hara fleeing the Atlanta fire

The Emerald City first appeared as a huge, sky-scraping palace

The watercolour storyboards helped the director visualize each scene

A WIZARD PRODUCTION

Every single scene of the children's classic *The Wizard of Oz* (1939) was drawn out on a storyboard first. These storyboards helped the director plan which scenes to shoot and how they should be framed. The colourful clothes of Dorothy, the Tin Man, and the Scarecrow were also worked out in detail so that they would blend in with the brightly painted matte backgrounds (pp. 16–17) of the Yellow Brick Road and the Emerald City.

Some storyboards were heavily annotated

CAMERA EFFECTS

They say that the camera never lies, but today's modern film cameras can perform a variety of tricks and special effects that change how and what the viewer sees. Gone are the days when the camera simply shot what was directly in front of it. Now a camera comes with a variety of optical lenses – fish-eye, wide-angle, zoom – that can be used to distort the picture. Special motor speeds either speed up or slow down the action. Custom-fitted harnesses make the camera seem weightless, so the operator can move around easily and change the camera's point of view at the director's whim. Modern cameras can also film underwater, and can even be attached to an air balloon and operated electronically from the sky. Whatever the future of the cinema, the most important aspect of moviemaking will always be that magic box, the film camera.

CONVENTIONAL 35 MM FILM

UNSQUEEZED ANAMORPHIC FILM

ALL KINDS OF SIZES

The most common type of film size is 35 mm, a standard format used in the majority of feature films today. Each frame follows the one before, and the strip of film travels down through the camera. However, by using a special anamorphic lens on the camera, a spectacular 180-degree widescreen effect can be achieved. Another anamorphic lens in the projector stretches the film out on the screen.

TRAVELLING AT HIGH SPEED

The first film cameras were operated by turning a handle on the side of a camera, which exposed the film. Modern cameras use motors that run film though the camera at 24 frames per second to create a normal running speed. For a scene that calls for something faster, such as this explosive sequence from *The Rock*, a director can use a speed of 12 frames per second which gives the scene a fast, jerky effect.

GOING SLOW

Many modern filmmakers like to use slow motion when shooting breathtaking action sequences. To do this the film has to be run through the camera at a much greater speed than normal to capture every minute detail of a fight sequence. Instead of the usual 24 frames per second, a director will use anything from 48 to 120 frames per second in the camera. When the film is shown, it is run through the projector at a much slower speed than normal. This technique was often used in films starring Jackie Chan or Bruce Lee. However, for Jackie Chan's fight scene (right) in *Rumble in the Bronx* (1995), a speed of 22 frames per second was used, which, when played back at normal speed, speeded up the action.

SPLIT-SCREEN IMAGES

Sometimes more than one image is needed to convey the action on screen. By using different images on the screen at the same time, directors can speed up the dramatic events of a film, link two people in different locations, or create suspense. They combine different sequences by using parallel editing, known as split-screen, and project them at the same time. This scene from the film *Grand Prix* shows three different events that are happening on the racetrack at the same time.

SPLIT-SCREEN IMAGES FROM *GRAND PRIX* (1966) WON THE FILM AN OSCAR FOR BEST EDITING

The fiery red echoes the relationship between the two characters

COLOURS OF THE RAINBOW

Sometimes a director of photography will use a special filter. A filter is a thin, coloured piece of glass which is fitted to the lens of the camera and absorbs a specific wavelength of light passing through it. In this scene from *Gone With the Wind* (above) a strong red filter is used to give the impression of a raging fire. Filters can be fully coloured to wash a scene in one particular colour, or they may be half-coloured to colour clouds and skylines on location shoots.

400 ft film magazine with running time of 4 1/4 minutes at normal speed

SPECIAL EFFECTS CAMERAS

As special effects directors became more demanding, movie cameras became more complex. Today's cameras can be fitted with a variety of special lenses, have mechanical motors, and can even be operated by remote control. Cameras such as this Arriflex 35 III have also become more compact and flexible to use. If they need to be mobile, camera operators can hand-hold the camera or it can be placed on a Steadicam (below).

Cameraman's eyepiece

Filters are placed in the filter tray

Prime lens interchangeable with zoom lenses

Black-and-white video assist camera

Locking knob to open or close camera door

Camera door is opened to thread the film past the gate

Stainless steels rods to support accessories such as a zoom lens

Matte box reduces lens flares

Follow focus control allows focus puller to precisely focus the lens

High-speed base plate allows cameraman to control precisely camera speeds from 5 to 120 frames per second

ARRIFLEX

Sylvester Stallone runs for his life across a rope bridge in Cliffhanger

STEADY AS THEY GO

The Steadicam is one of the great breakthroughs of modern moviemaking. Pioneered by Stanley Kubrick for his horror film *The Shining*, the Steadicam comes complete with a body harness which the cameraman wears while he holds the camera with a balancing steel pole. This balances the camera, giving the cameraman the illusion of the camera being weightless, and he can run without shaking the picture. The Steadicam can also be turned upside down to give a child's-eye view of the world.

The cameraman, filming with the Steadicam, is guided backwards

JAMES CAMERON

One of the most imaginative directors of his generation, James Cameron continues to astound his audiences with breathtaking films. A master of cinematography, Cameron gained global attention with the terrifying film *Aliens* (1989), before creating movie history in the special effects breakthrough *The Abyss* (1989), which used morphing techniques (pp. 58–59). His next film, *Terminator 2* (1992), used even more sophisticated special effects and became one of the biggest earning films of all time. His latest film, *Titanic* (1998), uses both the Steadicam and underwater cameras with spectacular success.

"He does mind us actors risking our lives for the shot, but he doesn't mind risking his own for the shot."
SIGOURNEY WEAVER

FILMING SFX

For special effects to look spectacular they must be filmed with the right equipment. Many special effects involve filming in difficult conditions for the camera operator, for example with water or fire on the set. Special watertight camera casings or covers for the camera make it possible to film underwater or in heavy rain, while zoom lenses mean that the camera crew can keep at a safe distance from fire or explosions. For different situations, different techniques are employed. Aerial shots or special stunts may need to be filmed using remote-control airborne cameras, while miniature models created in the studio can be made to look realistic by clever lighting and close-up camerawork.

Camera housed in protective casing

IN FLIGHT MOVIES

When action takes place in the air, or the director wants a bird's-eye view of action on the ground, the camera has to be airborne. A remote control camera can be fixed to the side of a helicopter and worked by the camera operator from inside. Films such as *Apocalypse Now* (1979) and *Top Gun* (1986) use this technique.

Camera is fitted with a zoom lens to "zoom" into the tunnel

Miniature ice tunnel lit by studio lights

Steel dolly track

EFFECTIVE IN THE STUDIO

When miniature models are photographed in the studio, a number of factors help create the illusion that they are life-size. Special lighting and a careful choice of camera and lens will play their part in creating the illusion that the viewer is travelling into an ice tunnel (above). Camera crews also often use dolly tracks – steel rails along which the camera can be made to run – so filming such close-ups runs smoothly and is perfectly timed.

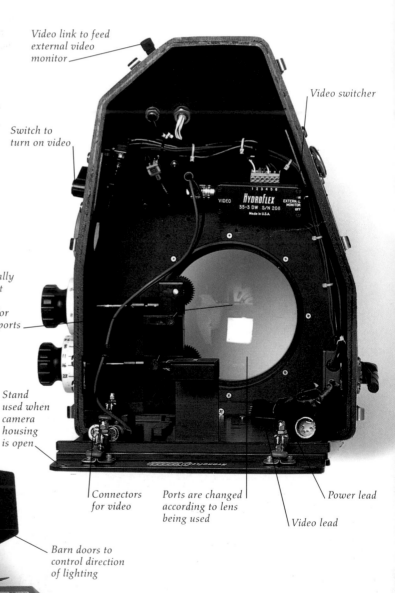

Video link to feed external video monitor

Video switcher

Switch to turn on video

Optically perfect glass used for front ports

Stand used when camera housing is open

Connectors for video

Ports are changed according to lens being used

Power lead

Video lead

Barn doors to control direction of lighting

Electronic power pack is sealed to prevent water damage

Power pack, which runs on 240 volts, is connected to mains

UNDERWATER LIGHTING

When filming underwater, special lighting is often required, particularly where the visibility is poor. Custom-made, waterproof lights take the place of sunbeams and light rays playing on the surface of the water, or shed light on the actors or fish swimming in the depths.

Sealed beam gas-filled bulb

HOT SHOTS

In the film *Backdraft* (1991), director Ron Howard placed his stars in the very heart of several burning buildings. The film crew kept their equipment at a safe distance, using zoom lenses to capture each scene, while pyrotechnic staff worked hard to ensure that the flames were controlled. The cameras were fitted with barn doors (below left) to prevent the brightness of the flames reflecting on the lens.

Sound operator on Hard Rain *makes sure his boom microphone does not get wet*

Camera crew huddled together at a safe distance on the set

GETTING WET

Filmmakers sometimes have to get wet when filming scenes such as this from *Hard Rain* (1998). A studio location was filled with water and the film crew had to manoeuvre their equipment above water, In this case a Steadicam is used because it can be held safely and easily above water level, while the actor, Christian Slater, and the rest of the crew, get wet in the interests of entertainment.

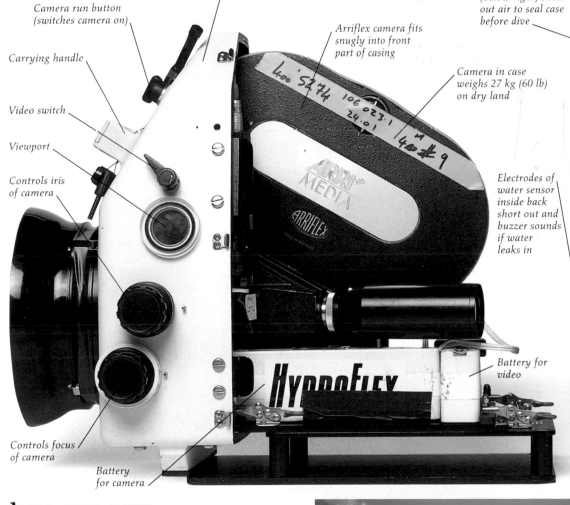

Camera run button (switches camera on)

Cast aluminium housing

Carrying handle

Arriflex camera fits snugly into front part of casing

Vacuum pump (below right) sucks out air to seal case before dive

Video switch

Camera in case weighs 27 kg (60 lb) on dry land

Viewport

Controls iris of camera

Electrodes of water sensor inside back short out and buzzer sounds if water leaks in

Handgrip

Battery for video

Controls focus of camera

Battery for camera

INTO THE DEEP

Normal studio cameras cannot film underwater. Instead, specially designed underwater camera casings are used by cameramen, such as Mike "Jaws" Valentine BSC (right), to hold the camera. The camera is encased in a special watertight container which is wired up to all the camera's usual facilities, such as the focus control and iris control. The case is buoyant in the water, and can be fully operated in deep water – up to a maximum depth of 55 m (150 ft).

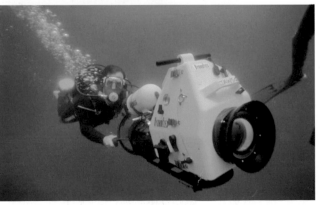

MIKE VALENTINE IN ACTION

UNDER PRESSURE

This air pump is used to pump all the air out of the camera casing before it is submerged. The lack of air creates a tight seal, so air must be pumped back in before the casing can be opened.

FIRST STEPS

Since the very beginnings of cinema in the mid-1890s, filmmakers have been striving to both improve and update the art of story-telling on camera. One technique that was developed early on was that of using special effects to bring fantastical or magical stories to life on screen. In early efforts such as *Voyage to the Moon* (1902) and *Journey into Space* (1905), French director Georges Méliès experimented with miniature models and camera perspectives. Effects animation (paintings superimposed onto film strips) and stop-motion photography (moving models one frame at a time) soon followed, before CGi took films into a new dimension.

STILL FROM *VOYAGE TO THE MOON*, BASED ON TWO NOVELS BY JULES VERNE

MÉLIÈS

The pioneer of special effects director Georges Méliès' first film, *The Conjuring of a Woman at the House of Roubert Houdin* (1896), shows a woman's head suspended over a candlestick. People crowded his privately-owned cinema to see more. Méliès was the first director to fully exploit miniature sets, stop-motion photography, and forced perspective in films. He even dared to push the boundaries of cinema underwater by filming his actors through an aquarium! His most famous film *Voyage to the Moon* (1902) was the first science-fiction blockbuster in motion picture history. The film lasted 13 minutes, comprised 30 different sets, and used explosives, matte paintings, and outsize sets.

Legend has it that Méliès discovered the art of special effects by accident. He got his exposed film trapped in the projector and noticed people disappearing and reappearing on screen.

Film of actor Todd Armstrong was combined with footage of skeletons

SKELETAL ANIMATION

Stop motion animation, achieved by stopping the camera between frames, was being used as long ago as the late 1800s. For *Jason and the Argonauts* (1963), the special effects model-maker Ray Harryhausen (pp. 22–23) opted for stop-motion photography to film a battle between model skeletons and real people. The skeletons were moved a tiny amount frame by frame, and the film combined with live action by an optical printer (p. 15).

A technician moves a Snow Walker one step forward during stop-motion photography

Each model was patiently moved one frame at a time during shooting

The warrior skeleton sequence took four and a half months to shoot

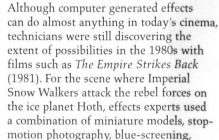

The planet Hoth was a miniature studio model, with baking soda for snow

SNOW WALKING

Although computer generated effects can do almost anything in today's cinema, technicians were still discovering the extent of possibilities in the 1980s with films such as *The Empire Strikes Back* (1981). For the scene where Imperial Snow Walkers attack the rebel forces on the ice planet Hoth, effects experts used a combination of miniature models, stop-motion photography, blue-screening, and hand-painted effects animation.

Large models were used for tight, close-up shots, while tiny Snow Walker models were used for extreme long shots

To avoid disturbing the snow, some Snow Walkers had to be manipulated from below the set, using camouflaged trap-doors

FINAL STILL FROM *THREE COINS IN A FOUNTAIN*

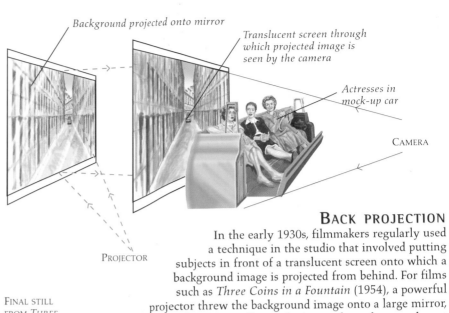

Background projected onto mirror

Translucent screen through which projected image is seen by the camera

Actresses in mock-up car

CAMERA

PROJECTOR

BACK PROJECTION

In the early 1930s, filmmakers regularly used a technique in the studio that involved putting subjects in front of a translucent screen onto which a background image is projected from behind. For films such as *Three Coins in a Fountain* (1954), a powerful projector threw the background image onto a large mirror, which in turn reflected the image through a translucent screen. The camera filmed the composited scene.

Background scene projected onto screen

STILL OF FINAL SCENE FROM *SUPERMAN*

Two-way mirror

CAMERA

PROJECTOR

Actor supported by hydraulic arm

Semi-transparent mirror

FRONT PROJECTION

The technique of front projection largely replaced back projection from the 1950s. The background image is projected from the front of the screen onto a semi-transparent mirror and then onto a two-way mirror, and the camera records the background and the foreground as one image. The film *Superman* (1978) used this method to give the illusion that actor Christopher Reeve flew above the city of Metropolis.

Camera films through the two-way mirror, blending background projection with the actor's image

Camera and projector were synchronized, so when the camera zoomed in on the actor, the background also zoomed

Movie camera re-photographs the films loaded into each projector

Actors Dick Van Dyke and Julie Andrews take time out for a day at the races in Mary Poppins

Cartoon characters were painted directly on a cel

Optical printer joins sequences shot at different times and in different places

Printer contains two to four projectors which run the different film strips

DANCING TO SUCCESS

Disney's *Mary Poppins* (1964) successfully combined live action with hand-painted animation. The tale of the "practically perfect" nanny used ground-breaking effects to show Julie Andrews, Dick Van Dyke, Karen Dotrice, and Matthew Garber walking and dancing through an animated landscape. The animators drew the cartoons on special sheets of celluloid known as "cels", which were then laid over large prints made of the live-action film so that the animated characters could "interact" with the actors.

STILL FROM THE OSCAR-WINNING FILM *MARY POPPINS*

OPTICAL PRINTER

MATTE PAINTING

From the beginning, Hollywood filmmakers have tried to create the illusion of vast open spaces by filming massive panoramic views behind their film stars. Early pioneers literally painted these wonderful backgrounds by using two-dimensional paintings on glass called mattes, which were then blended into the live-action footage. This was made possible by blacking out particular areas of film and filling these areas with a background painting. Matte paintings have been used by film directors from Orson Welles to Steven Spielberg. Instead of taking up extra time and spending more money travelling to distant locations, or building expensive sets and miniature models, an experienced matte painter can create the desired effect in the studio. Today, there are not as many matte painters because it is possible to create backgrounds digitally with a computer (pp. 54–55).

TECHNICAL WIZARDRY

One of the first films to explore the possibilities of matte painting was *The Wizard of Oz* (1939). The script called for several spectacular scenes, including a never-ending yellow brick road and the sky-scraping Emerald City. Director Victor Fleming filmed his actors in a studio, leaving enough room in the frame for a matte painting to be blended in later. The colourful paintings were then combined with the studio negatives to create a magical fantasy world.

Architectural features from classical buildings were used as reference

RESEARCHING AND REFERENCING

Before any matte paintings are created, designers must first decide what needs to be painted, and then find reference for the background that is to be painted. For the film *Batman* (1989), the designers decided to create Gotham City as a very dark, gothic environment. For the matte painting sequence (right), they based their designs on gothic cathedrals and museums found in Europe.

1 CREATING THE MATTE

Director Tim Burton's fantasy Gotham City came to life by means of several matte paintings. The strange architecture of the mattes was blended with real-life footage of busy street scenes. For this one, a studio back-lot was set up as a normal city avenue at night. The top of the scene was then blacked out, so that a matte painting could be drawn.

2 PAINTING ON GLASS

Using the references (bottom left), the matte painting was then painted onto glass and made to fit the exact measurements of the "blacked out" area of the original studio shot. The blacked out area marks the top of filmed buildings that will appear in the finished shot, and the matte artist had to be careful not to paint down beyond them.

It is impossible to see where the studio shot ends and the matte painting begins

3 COMBINING IMAGES

The combination of the studio film and the matte painting has created this very powerful image of Gotham City. The normal studio footage has been blended effortlessly with the matte painting in post production. The incredible matte paintings created for the film *Batman* helped Anton Furst, the film's production designer, win an Oscar.

Lividly coloured sky created by combination of matte painting and computer graphics

Blacked out area to be replaced by matte painting

THE VILLAGE CONVENT WAS FILMED AT A SPECIAL ANGLE TO FIT IN WITH THE MATTE

THE LEFT SIDE OF THE NEGATIVE IS "BLACKED OUT" TO MAKE WAY FOR THE MATTE PAINTING

FUTURE WORLD

For the film *The Fifth Element* (1997), designers were asked to create a futuristic New York skyline where the Earth's sea level had completely dropped. This matte painting shows the Statue of Liberty towering on a pinnacle of rock, while the Brooklyn Bridge hovers hundreds of metres above the ground. Spacecraft were later added using computer graphics.

TRICKS OF THE TRADE

Director Michael Powell recreated a remote village in the Himalayas on the sound stages of Pinewood Studios, England, for his film *Black Narcissus* (1947). The paintings for the film included gigantic caverns and vertical cliff faces, structures that would have been impossible to film in the difficult terrain of the Himalayan mountains.

A MATTE PAINTING OF A HIMALAYAN CLIFFTOP IS THEN BLENDED WITH THE STUDIO FILM FOR THE FINISHED SHOT

Photographs of Tibetan villages and mountains act as reference for the artist

Meticulous attention to detail makes village look real

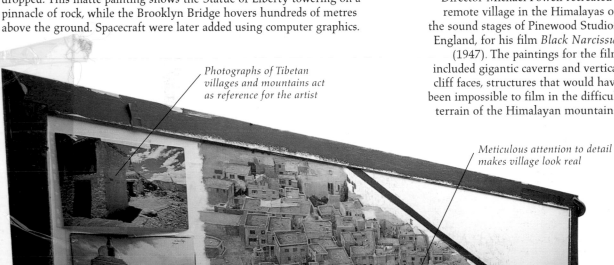

THE FUTURE FOR MATTE

Although computer graphics are replacing matte paintings in films, many directors believe that paintings provide more detail and, sometimes, greater flexibility. For *Seven Years in Tibet* (1997), studio designers decided to use a matte painting of a Tibetan village for a sequence. The camera travelled down the length of the matte and off to the bottom left-hand side, as if taking aerial shots of a real village.

BLUE SCREEN, GREEN SCREEN

If a director wants an actor to hang from the Empire State Building or zip through an asteroid belt in outer space, the optical trickery of the blue or green screen technique can be used to achieve the apparently impossible. An actor or model is filmed in front of a pure blue- or green-lit screen using colour negative film which is invisible to photography's primary colours – red, blue, and green. The image can then be isolated from the blue background by masking or blanking out the blue or green. Until the early 1990s the masking out was done by an optical printer (pp. 14–15), but today, special software allows the image to be manipulated digitally and makes the process much more versatile. The background colour can be replaced with a matte painting, or live action film of a raging fire, huge waterfall, or even the surface of Mars.

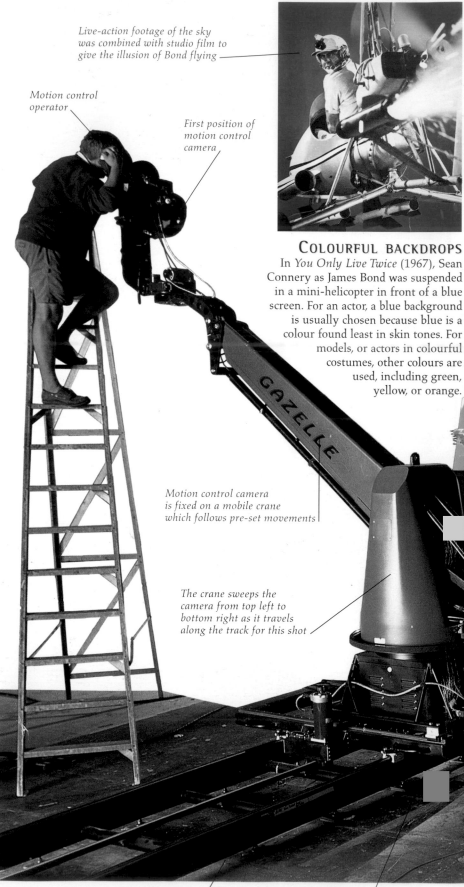

Live-action footage of the sky was combined with studio film to give the illusion of Bond flying

Motion control operator

First position of motion control camera

COLOURFUL BACKDROPS
In *You Only Live Twice* (1967), Sean Connery as James Bond was suspended in a mini-helicopter in front of a blue screen. For an actor, a blue background is usually chosen because blue is a colour found least in skin tones. For models, or actors in colourful costumes, other colours are used, including green, yellow, or orange.

Motion control camera is fixed on a mobile crane which follows pre-set movements

The crane sweeps the camera from top left to bottom right as it travels along the track for this shot

BLUE SCREEN ON LOCATION
Blue-screen projections are not always used in an indoor studio. Sometimes a special effects sequence will call for an outdoor shot, such as this scene from *Con Air*. Instead of using a miniature model, the producers decided to shoot a military attack using a real helicopter and real actors in front of a huge blue screen. By working outdoors, technicians were able to use natural lighting for the helicopter, which helped to make the airborne attack realistic.

IN THE GREEN STUDIO
Different coloured screens are used, depending on the colours of the subject being shot. The technicians working on the film *Lost in Space* (1998) decided to use a green screen to contrast with the silvery blue spacecraft. A motion control camera, controlled by a computer, executes exactly the same sequence of movements several times while moving along a steel track. Each sequence is known as a "pass" and picks up different elements of the scene. These will then be put together digitally with the separately filmed background.

Great care is taken to ensure that the steel track is absolutely level so that the camera runs smoothly

Some stop motion shots require the camera to glide many metres along a track

1 BLUE SCREEN LIVE ACTION

For the film *Memoirs of an Invisible Man* (1992), actor Chevy Chase had to be made to disappear. Chevy Chase wore a special blue bodysuit during shooting, and by updating the visual trickery first used in 1990 for *Ghost,* special effects experts were able to erase the actor's body piece by piece, keeping the clothing.

2 DIGITAL MANIPULATION

The blue bodysuit worn by Chevy Chase was digitally removed by computer in post production. The technicians also used digital manipulation to enhance the 3–D effect of the actor's clothing. In the film, the blue-screen technique is successfully used to make it appear that an invisible man is involved in a variety of activities.

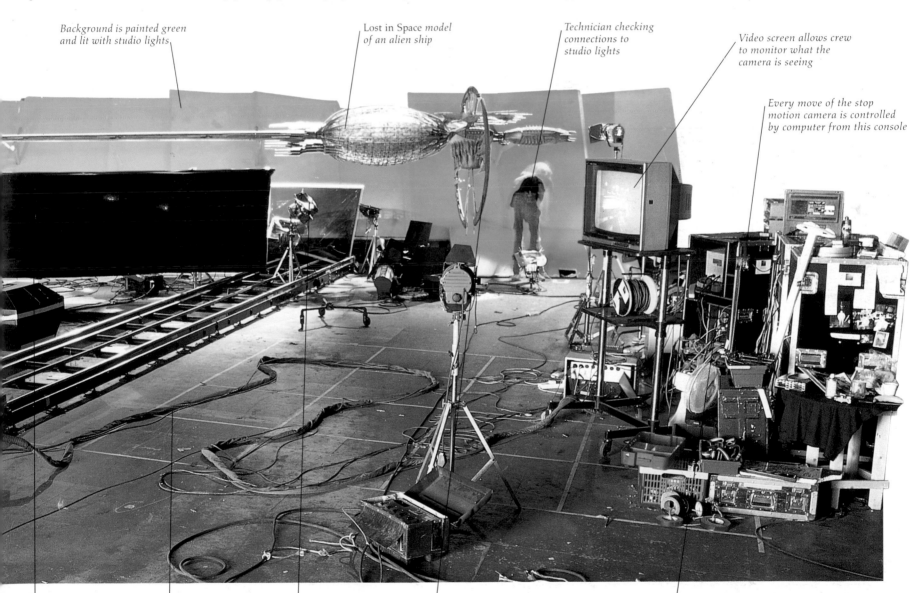

Background is painted green and lit with studio lights

Lost in Space model of an alien ship

Technician checking connections to studio lights

Video screen allows crew to monitor what the camera is seeing

Every move of the stop motion camera is controlled by computer from this console

Black screen to stop the flare from studio lights hitting camera lens

Cable connecting camera to computer controls

Lights covered in coloured gel to give purple/blue tinge to model

Small lights on model will be filmed on their own in one of the passes by the camera

Several technicians, including the motion control operator, sit behind this bank of machinery, controlling and monitoring the camera's passes

A matte painting shows distant planets in a far-away galaxy

The X-wings that are so impressive on screen were tiny models

The Death Star – one of the most popular models built for the film

Each fighter was individually shot and duplicated on screen to create an army

IN SPACE

Space – the final frontier. No other subject in the film world generates as much excitement and wonder as science fiction. From the very beginnings of cinema, directors like George Méliès were creating futuristic films such as *Voyage to the Moon* (1902), preparing the ground for future filmmakers such as George Lucas with his *Star Wars* trilogy, and Steven Spielberg with *Close Encounters of the Third Kind* (1977) and *E.T. the Extra-Terrestrial* (1982). Special and visual effects have made it possible for audiences to gaze out at the stars, discover new planets and strange creatures, and watch spectacular battles being fought across the galaxy. Sometimes the special effect is created by surprising methods – flying a model spaceship in a water tank, or using miniature models no bigger than a thumbnail. And innovative directors and special effects departments continue to develop new methods to create more spectacular effects for films set in future times and distant places.

MODELLING SPACECRAFT

Spacecraft come in all shapes and sizes. For *Star Wars* (1977) alone, there were life-size models of Han Solo's Millennium Falcon and miniscule replicas of the rebel X-wing fighters (above). Designers built the spacecrafts to different sizes depending on where the camera was positioned. A close-up required a very large, detailed model of a ship, showing all its gadgets and lights. A long shot, such as the Snow Walker attack in *The Empire Strikes Back* (1980) used miniature models against a fake background.

The astronaut, suspended from wires in the studio, used slow body movements to portray weightlessness

SCENE FROM *2001: A SPACE ODYSSEY*

SPACE WALKING

Directors have tried a variety of methods to reproduce the effects of weightlessness in space, from high-wire techniques to rear projection (pp. 14–15). Today, most directors suspend the actor in front of a blue screen, shoot the scene with slow-motion control cameras, and then combine the image with a star-filled background.

GEORGE LUCAS

Although it is more than 20 years since he wrote and directed *Star Wars* (1977), George Lucas remains one of the most powerful people working in the film industry. Obsessed with science fiction, Lucas has influenced the development of space films more than anyone else and continues to dazzle and astound movie audiences around the world with his ground-breaking special effects. He created the world-famous Industrial Light & Magic (ILM) SFX company in 1975 and has been involved as producer with the biggest blockbusters of all time, including *Raiders of the Lost Ark*. He is currently filming three *Star Wars* prequel movies which promise to take cinema into the 21st century.

"George has never stopped asking the question 'Any ideas?'"
STEVEN SPIELBERG

"One of the reasons I started doing Star Wars *was that I was interested in creating a new kind of myth, and using space to do it because it is the new frontier."*

CREATING GRAVITY

One of the main difficulties of shooting space films is the problem of how to show zero gravity. For his film *2001: A Space Odyssey* (1969), Stanley Kubrick decided to build a life-size gravity machine to give the illusion of weightlessness. The entire set of the spacecraft was attached to a camera hoist and both rotated on a gyroscope while the actor remained stationary. This clever apparatus gives the illusion in the film of the astronaut floating around the spaceship as it revolves in space.

FLYING IN A CLOUD TANK

To show a spaceship hurtling through the cosmos it is possible to simply float a model in a water tank! SFX experts have designed a special "cloud tank" filled with water which, when specially lit, gives the illusion of space travel. Clouds made with kapok – a material usually used to stuff cushions – are floated in the water, and white paint siphoned in to make the clouds look smoky. The tank is lit from underneath as well as from the side, and a high-speed camera shoots the entire process in close-up.

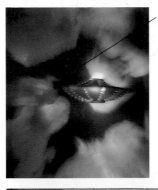

Fast film creates zoom effect

The angle of the spaceship can be altered

Different coloured gels create different lighting effects

CGi effects add to the cloud tank illusion

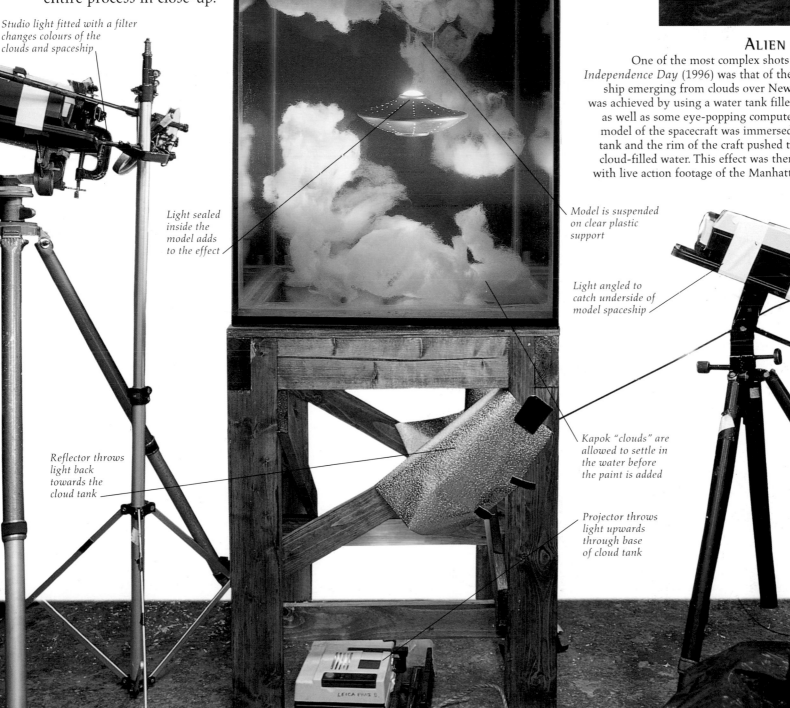

Studio light fitted with a filter changes colours of the clouds and spaceship

Light sealed inside the model adds to the effect

Reflector throws light back towards the cloud tank

Model is suspended on clear plastic support

Light angled to catch underside of model spaceship

Kapok "clouds" are allowed to settle in the water before the paint is added

Projector throws light upwards through base of cloud tank

ALIEN CLOUDS

One of the most complex shots of the film *Independence Day* (1996) was that of the Destroyer ship emerging from clouds over New York. This was achieved by using a water tank filled with dye, as well as some eye-popping computer effects. A model of the spacecraft was immersed in a water tank and the rim of the craft pushed through the cloud-filled water. This effect was then combined with live action footage of the Manhattan skyline.

MAKING IT MOVE

From King Kong wreaking havoc in downtown New York (1933) to a T Rex attacking the streets of San Diego in *The Lost World* (1997), filmmakers have relied on the creative skills of puppeteers and animatronic experts. A range of techniques are employed to bring such monster creations to life. One early method of animation was "stop-motion" where the puppet is moved and filmed frame by frame. Other techniques include operating puppets by rods, which are light, flexible and can be moved quickly. Modern puppeteers now favour "go-motion", a system which moves the puppet with rods that are computer-controlled, and the ground-breaking Dinosaur Input Device (DID). First used in *Jurassic Park* (1993), DID mixes stop-motion animation with computer graphics technology.

GODZILLA
The fire-breathing lizard Godzilla has always been a favourite among puppeteers. Japan's answer to the sci-fi craze in the West burst on the scene in *Godzilla, King of the Monsters* (1955). Modelmakers used stop-motion photography and a variety of miniature models to depict the destructive but popular creature.

Every hair was individually inserted to make Buddy look realistic

Each limb has its own separate control rod

Rods carrying wiring lead up the back of the puppet to work the limbs

Servo connector links up with the computer control to supply body movements

MONKEY MECHANICS
For the film *Buddy* (1997), a life-size gorilla was constructed using traditional puppetry materials and state-of-the-art animatronic gadgets. On the surface, the baby gorilla looks incredibly lifelike, with skin, hair, teeth, and hands. Inside, however, is an intricate mechanical control system which operates the arms, legs, and facial expressions. Rods and cables connect the internal mechanics to the puppeteers' controls.

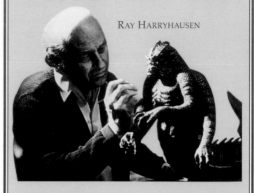
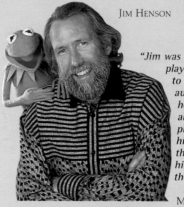
A "blow-tube" inflates the gorilla's cheeks slightly to make the puppet breathe

Pressure pad for operating lips and tongue

SERVO CONNECTOR

CONTROL FOR BUDDY'S LEFT HAND

CONTROL FOR BUDDY'S RIGHT HAND

CONTROL FOR BUDDY'S LEFT FOOT

CONTROL FOR BUDDY'S RIGHT FOOT

TAKING A WALK

For the film *The Adventures of Pinocchio* (1996) a variety of special effects were used to bring Gepetto's wooden marionette to life. For Pinocchio to walk through the streets, a complex walking rig was constructed with a pole arm supporting the "wooden" puppet. Technicians followed the puppet and operated its leg movements with a variety of mechanical poles attached to Pinocchio's back.

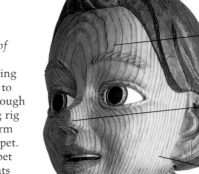

The face was made from foam latex and painted to look like wood

Different noses were manipulated onto the puppet's face using computer-generated effects

Facial expressions were operated by remote control using a motor encased in Pinocchio's head

Mechanical rod attached to an animatronic motor in Pinocchio's body operates arms, legs, and neck movements

Puppeteers stay out of shot while making Pinocchio "walk" with mechanical rods

Special Ultimatt blue suits were worn by the puppeteers

Animatronic motor fits snugly in fibreglass body

BLUE SCREEN TECHNIQUES

Blue-screen technology was used where the full-bodied Pinocchio appeared on screen with live actors. Puppeteers dressed in blue suits in front of a blue screen operated the puppet using blue rods. Later, in post production, all the blue elements were digitally removed and replaced with background footage of streets. This combination of blue screen and puppetry brought Pinocchio to life without the need for wires or steel rigs.

Technicians worked for months to get Pinocchio's body movements just right

Actors have to imagine the scenery when working with blue screen

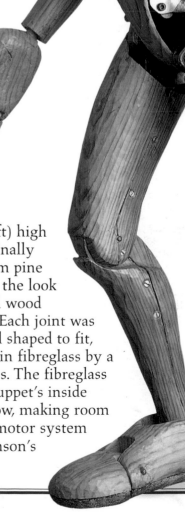

Puppeteers operate blue-screen rods

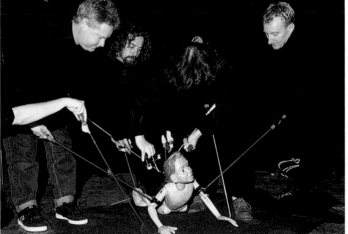

BLUE RODS

Twelve separate Pinocchio puppets were built and a total of ten puppeteers were involved in operating them. Using the latest in puppet animation technology, Pinocchio had the capacity to do everything from running through a forest to eating a cream-puff cake in a bakery. Here technicians are operating the puppet as it crawls along the floor. Blue-screen rods were used to move the puppet's arms, legs, and head. The rods were later digitally removed to make Pinocchio's movements look seamless in the film.

PINOCCHIO

The 0.8-m (2.7-ft) high puppet was originally hand-carved from pine wood to provide the look and feel of a real wood chipped puppet. Each joint was precisely cut and shaped to fit, and then copied in fibreglass by a moulding process. The fibreglass model left the puppet's inside completely hollow, making room for an intricate motor system built by Jim Henson's Creature Shop.

ANIMATING ANIMALS

No actor finds it easy to work with animals but the magic of today's cinema makes it easier for actors to share the screen amicably with dinosaurs, dragons, aliens, and gorillas. This is possible because of animatronics, the process of creating electronic and mechanical creatures that respond to remote control signals. Animatronics can create the unbelievable without the need for special trainers or re-takes, and the creatures can take the shape of ordinary animals, such as the gorilla in the film *Buddy* (1997), or fantastic aliens and monsters from outer space. Bringing animal robots to life, however, takes months of preparation by skilled craftspeople and puppeteers. On the set, the models and costumes are strapped and harnessed with wires, rods, metal frames, and electronic sensors that together create the illusion of a living, breathing animal, with realistic skin, hair, teeth, and claws.

DRESSING THE PART

Imitating a living animal can often lead to monkey business! For the film *Buddy*, four different model gorillas were built to show the hero of the movie as a baby, a toddler, a juvenile, and an adult ape. For the adult version an actor wears a padded muscle suit covered by an authentic "hair" suit.

The muscle suit is custom-built to fit the actor

The adult head is fully animatronic and worn like a crash helmet

It took one person six weeks to punch in all the hairs on Buddy's back

Velcro straps attach the ape feet to the body of the suit

The flexible rubber hands fit like gloves

The "hair" suit is put on over the muscle suit – the heat inside is intense!

ANIMATING AN ANIMATRONIC APE HEAD

All animals convey emotion with their faces. For *Buddy*, the animatronic head was made to convey an array of emotions with its eyes, nose, mouth, and facial muscles. Model-makers at Jim Henson's Creature Shop developed an intricate head from observation of live gorillas. The animatronic head was worn by an actor for close-ups in the movie, and every twitch of its features was operated by remote control.

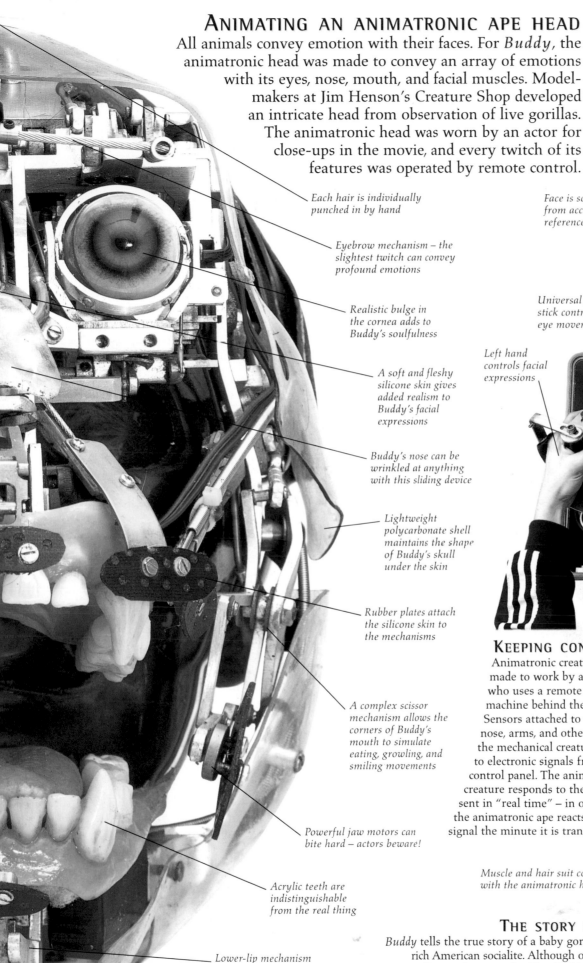

Each hair is individually punched in by hand

Eyebrow mechanism – the slightest twitch can convey profound emotions

Realistic bulge in the cornea adds to Buddy's soulfulness

A soft and fleshy silicone skin gives added realism to Buddy's facial expressions

Buddy's nose can be wrinkled at anything with this sliding device

Lightweight polycarbonate shell maintains the shape of Buddy's skull under the skin

Rubber plates attach the silicone skin to the mechanisms

A complex scissor mechanism allows the corners of Buddy's mouth to simulate eating, growling, and smiling movements

Powerful jaw motors can bite hard – actors beware!

Acrylic teeth are indistinguishable from the real thing

Lower-lip mechanism

MOULDING THE MODEL

Sculpting and moulding are important aspects of animatronics. A model is sculpted in non-drying clay which can be worked on and blended easily without cracking. When the sculpture is complete, a mould of it is made in fibreglass. The mould is then cast in silicone or foam latex (see pp. 34–35).

Face is sculpted from accurate reference

Universal joy stick controls eye movements

Cable connects puppet to control rig

Mitten control is adapted from traditional puppetry

Left hand controls facial expressions

Commands can be programmed in on site

Right hand controls mouth movements

KEEPING CONTROL

Animatronic creations are made to work by an operator who uses a remote control machine behind the camera. Sensors attached to the eyes, nose, arms, and other parts of the mechanical creature respond to electronic signals from the control panel. The animatronic creature responds to the messages sent in "real time" – in other words, the animatronic ape reacts to the signal the minute it is transmitted.

Muscle and hair suit combined with the animatronic head

THE STORY OF BUDDY

Buddy tells the true story of a baby gorilla raised by a rich American socialite. Although often dressed as a human being in the film, Buddy's movements and actions still had to be recognizably those of an ape, so animal experts were always on hand during filming in Los Angeles to give advice.

LARGER THAN LIFE

SHRUNK TO FIT
One of the most innovative films to use outsize sets was the 1957 classic *The Incredible Shrinking Man*. Actor Grant Williams shrinks to micro-size after being caught in a radioactive mist. The ground-breaking visual effects used a mixture of outsize models and matte paintings to blend the actor into lifesize footage of kitchen floors and tables.

VOYAGE OF DISCOVERY
In the 1966 film blockbuster *Fantastic Voyage*, Stephen Boyd and Raquel Welch travel through the bloodstream of a sick man, after being shrunk and injected into his arm. The film used state-of-the-art back projections (p. 15) to portray the vast interiors of the human body, and won Oscars for visual effects and set decoration.

Filmed background is added to actor's blue screen image

TALL TALES
When the Jonathan Swift novel *Gulliver's Travels* was turned into a big budget television drama, the latest technology was used to bring to life both the tiny island of Lilliput and the giant world of Brobdingnag. Special sets were created to scale to make actor Ted Danson look minute in Brobdingnag, while blue-screen projections were used to show Danson towering above the miniscule Lilliputians.

If you were just 10 cm (4 ins) high, floorboards would stretch out like giant motorways, chairs would look like towering skyscrapers, and friendly family pets would turn into terrifying monsters. Hollywood has always been fascinated by the notion of small people, and has created imaginative films like *Honey, I Shrunk the Kids* where pocket-sized children trek across their garden, avoiding bumble bees, hosepipes, and the deadly lawn-mower along the way. To create such effects, various techniques are used, including outsize sets, giant props and the use of blue screen.

HANGIN' IN THERE
When miniature people have to appear to perform hair-raising stunts, the actors are often filmed in front of a blue screen projection which will later be replaced by background footage (pp.18–19). One stunt for the film *The Borrowers* involved Jim Broadbent climbing down a kitchen shelf using a paper clip and some sewing thread. The sequence was shot on a studio sound stage using a giant tea cup prop.

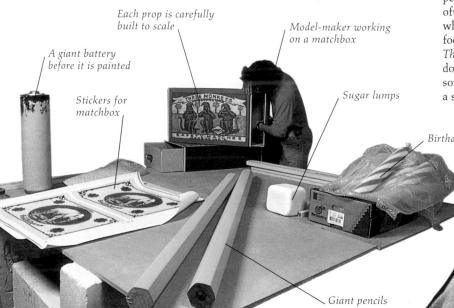

Each prop is carefully built to scale

Model-maker working on a matchbox

A giant battery before it is painted

Stickers for matchbox

Sugar lumps

Birthday candles

Giant pencils

LARGE PROPS FOR LITTLE PEOPLE
To create outsize props for the magical small world of the film *The Borrowers* (1997), the production designers had to build giant props to scale. Each ordinary object had to be constructed as it would have been seen or used by a little person only 10 cm (4 in) tall, so it was very important to use household items that would have interesting shapes when enlarged 14 times. The giant props (above) were created from polystyrene and foam and then painted.

IT'S A SMALL WORLD
Adapted from Mary Norton's famous children's books, *The Borrowers* tells the story of the Clock family, a group of tiny people who live under the floorboards of a big house and survive by "borrowing" things from the human family upstairs. The film contains a dazzling array of special effects which blend together the ordinary-sized world of the Borrowers and the huge outsize world of the house they inhabit. For the kitchen sequences, giant props were made by model-makers.

Faithfully re-created giant pepper mill painted to look like it is made from wood

China-effect sugar shaker with Pod Clock's homemade climbing gear hanging from it

Bendy drinking straws were made from lightweight plastic

A giant sticky sweet is among the many "borrowed" items collected by the Clocks

IN MINIATURE

The art of miniature model-making has always been an important aspect of special effects in cinema. When storylines call for volcanic eruptions, explosions on the Golden Gate Bridge or an armed force charging through the desert, location managers can save time and money by producing miniature models for these scenes. The next four pages follow the story of the building of a miniature landscape for a television documentary. To create the illusion of a prehistoric world, a special effects team built a large-scale landscape in the workshop. They also made models of early reptiles which needed to be moved around, and so were designed to be operated from underneath the construction.

FLYING HIGH
One of the most memorable images in modern cinema is the shot of Elliot riding his bicycle past the moon in *E.T. The Extra-terrestrial* (1982). To create the scene, a blue-screen shot of actor Henry Thomas on the bicycle in the studio was miniaturized and blended with a miniature model of the moon rising above the forest.

1 FIRST IMPRESSIONS
Before the miniature landscape is constructed the model-makers build a "concept" model. This model gives a general view of what the finished model will look like. This 0.4m x 0.4m (1ft x 1ft) model shows that the landscape will include a fallen tree and a circular lake.

3 GETTING STARTED
Constructing the 8.7 m x 8.7 m (24 ft x 24 ft) miniature model itself requires team effort. The base material for the model is polystyrene, and the model-makers have to carve out the detail using references such as pictures of trees and rock structures, and, in this case, photographs of a dry river bed. They also need to make the individual trees and bushes that will be added to the landscape later.

Model-makers carve details in ground of model's front section

Miniature trees and bushes are modelled with plastic and paint, as well real pieces of greenery

CARVING IT OUT 4
Here, the model-makers are cutting out the area of the huge circular lake at the heart of the model. They will then add more surface detail and mark out other features in the landscape. For example, the miniature trees built for the model are used as reference for the model-makers as they position holes in the polystyrene.

2 GETTING LARGER
When the shape and size of the concept model is agreed, the model-makers build a more detailed "prototype" model to give a clearer picture of the elements of the final model, and to show which sections are to be fitted together. This 0.6 m x 0.6 m (2 ft x 2 ft) prototype model is fully painted and fitted with shrubs and trees. When the prototype has been agreed, the team move on to build the full-size miniature model and its component pieces.

Card representation of early reptile

Final model landscape will be in three main sections – white areas show where the divides are between the main sections

REBUILDING 5
The miniature model is cut into agreed sections with hot wire so that it can be readily taken apart and transported to the film studio. Because it is so large and detailed, the sections of landscape are numbered as they are cut up for transportation. This is so that they can be re-assembled easily when the pieces reach the film studio.

Rebuilding the landscape is just like putting a huge jigsaw together

6 FOAMING THE MODEL

When the modelling of the landscape is complete, and all surface detail added, a technician wearing a special protective suit and mask sprays the entire model with a light foam made from toxic industrial chemicals. This foam gives the surface of the model a smooth, natural look, and adds bumps and dips to the surface to make it look just like a real landscape.

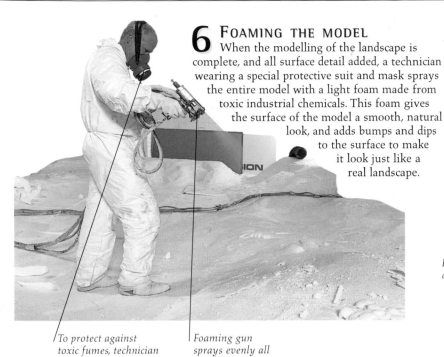

To protect against toxic fumes, technician wears a face mask

Foaming gun sprays evenly all over the surface

IN THE STUDIO 7

Rebuilding the landscape miniature and putting the final touches to it in the studio requires immense attention to detail. The entire landscape was separated into three main sections, the foreground section being the largest. A huge, panoramic backdrop of blue sky streaked with clouds was placed on the far wall of the studio to give depth and perspective, and studio lighting positioned above to give the landscape more texture and shadow.

Technician's head pops up between two of the main landscape sections

Appropriate large potted plants are used for the foreground

An ordinary hairdryer is used to seal glued sections

8 FIXING IN PLACE

When the landscape has been pieced together, the model-makers uses a special sealant glue to stick one section to another. The glue is dried with a hairdryer because this can be easily controlled and is directional, so it will not disturb other delicate details of the landscape's surface.

A monitor shows the technician what the landscape looks like from the camera's perspective

A reptile is undisturbed by the technician's activities

REPTILE MODELLING

Early reptiles were needed to inhabit the prehistoric scene, so miniature models of were prepared. After it was agreed which reptiles to model, including Moschops (below), each one was sculpted carefully in non-drying clay, which is easy to shape. The model is attached to metal leg stands, and the smallest details are added at this stage, including horned backbones, razor-sharp claws, and scaled reptile skin.

Model-maker adds detail to the reptile's skin

Finished sculpted clay reptile

When the sculpted clay reptile is finished, it is left to dry. The model-makers can then photograph the model from every possible angle to test whether the creature will look convincing in a 3-D environment. When they are satisfied, they move to the next stage, which is to create a mould of the reptile, which can then be used to cast several final foam latex models.

The model-maker sprays the model with plastic sealer to make it possible to release the fibreglass of the mould from the clay later on. A dividing wall of clay is then placed round the model (right) so that when the mould is made it can be split into two halves.

Foam latex model of a Lystrosaur

The mould is filled with foam latex and the result is this white-faced reptile. The model-makers can now paint its skin with different textures of green and yellow. The creature is hollow in the middle so that SFX technicians can get their arms up and inside to operate it without the viewer seeing.

Water makes Lystrosaur glisten on film

The final image of one reptile perched on a fallen log in the miniature landscape looks incredibly realistic. The creature has also been given small eyes, pointed claws, and fanged teeth. Before the cameras roll, the miniature reptile is sprayed with water.

continued on next page...

FINALLY SET

It has taken most of the day for the full set to be put together, and only the finishing touches remain to be added. The set is raised off the ground, so that the SFX technicians can get underneath to move the model reptiles around when needed. The background section is much smaller than the detailed foreground section to give the scene the effect of rolling away into the distance. The large painted backdrop and studio lighting add to the illusion of a vast prehistoric savannah roamed by early reptiles.

TRICKS OF THE TRADE

The model-makers go to great lengths to make a miniature look as realistic as possible. Part of the back section of this landscape was modelled with a slight depression to be filled with water only to a depth of 4 cm (1.5 in), to keep the amount of water on set to a minimum. Here, the model-makers are layering the pond with muslin fabric so it will look more like a lake, and give the illusion of being much deeper.

Model-makers refer to television monitor for camera's eye-view

Miniature trees are planted in the section behind muslin-coated pond

Large, potted trees are used for foreground section

Real log is used in foreground of landscape

Faithfully re-created giant pepper mill painted to look like it is made from wood

China-effect sugar shaker with Pod Clock's homemade climbing gear hanging from it

Bendy drinking straws were made from lightweight plastic

A giant sticky sweet is among the many "borrowed" items collected by the Clocks

IN MINIATURE

The art of miniature model-making has always been an important aspect of special effects in cinema. When storylines call for volcanic eruptions, explosions on the Golden Gate Bridge or an armed force charging through the desert, location managers can save time and money by producing miniature models for these scenes. The next four pages follow the story of the building of a miniature landscape for a television documentary. To create the illusion of a prehistoric world, a special effects team built a large-scale landscape in the workshop. They also made models of early reptiles which needed to be moved around, and so were designed to be operated from underneath the construction.

FLYING HIGH

One of the most memorable images in modern cinema is the shot of Elliot riding his bicycle past the moon in *E.T. The Extra-terrestrial* (1982). To create the scene, a blue-screen shot of actor Henry Thomas on the bicycle in the studio was miniaturized and blended with a miniature model of the moon rising above the forest.

1 FIRST IMPRESSIONS

Before the miniature landscape is constructed the model-makers build a "concept" model. This model gives a general view of what the finished model will look like. This 0.4m x 0.4m (1ft x 1ft) model shows that the landscape will include a fallen tree and a circular lake.

2 GETTING LARGER

When the shape and size of the concept model is agreed, the model-makers build a more detailed "prototype" model to give a clearer picture of the elements of the final model, and to show which sections are to be fitted together. This 0.6 m x 0.6 m (2 ft x 2 ft) prototype model is fully painted and fitted with shrubs and trees. When the prototype has been agreed, the team move on to build the full-size miniature model and its component pieces.

Card representation of early reptile

3 GETTING STARTED

Constructing the 8.7 m x 8.7 m (24 ft x 24 ft) miniature model itself requires team effort. The base material for the model is polystyrene, and the model-makers have to carve out the detail using references such as pictures of trees and rock structures, and, in this case, photographs of a dry river bed. They also need to make the individual trees and bushes that will be added to the landscape later.

Model-makers carve details in ground of model's front section

Miniature trees and bushes are modelled with plastic and paint, as well real pieces of greenery

CARVING IT OUT 4

Here, the model-makers are cutting out the area of the huge circular lake at the heart of the model. They will then add more surface detail and mark out other features in the landscape. For example, the miniature trees built for the model are used as reference for the model-makers as they position holes in the polystyrene.

Final model landscape will be in three main sections – white areas show where the divides are between the main sections

Rebuilding the landscape is just like putting a huge jigsaw together

REBUILDING 5

The miniature model is cut into agreed sections with hot wire so that it can be readily taken apart and transported to the film studio. Because it is so large and detailed, the sections of landscape are numbered as they are cut up for transportation. This is so that they can be re-assembled easily when the pieces reach the film studio.

TOY SOLDIERS

When the character Indiana Jones finds himself on the trail of the holy Ark of the Covenant for the film *Raiders of the Lost Ark* (1981), he discovers an army of German soldiers already excavating the site of the Ark's burial in the desert. Director Steven Spielberg used a miniature model built in the studio to plan the panoramic shots. Directors often use art department models to plan the way a scene should look, including actors' movements, the scenery, and any special lighting or camera angles.

Spielberg decides where to position the camera for the desert shot

Sand dunes are constructed from polystyrene and beach sand

Miniature models of tents, tanks and other vehicles were used

Tiny toy soldiers were used to represent the German army

Model-maker advises on placing of final greenery on miniature

Reptiles will be operated from underneath the platform

Landscape is supported on timber platform

Sand used on ground of miniature and to cover cracks in model surface

Model was fitted with dolls-house furniture so the debris flying out would look realistic

CGi effects were blended with the model White House

FINAL STILL OF THE WHITE HOUSE BEING DESTROYED IN *INDEPENDENCE DAY*

EXPLOSIVE MODELS

One of the most explosive sequences in the film *Independence Day* (1996) was when the alien ship destroys the White House in Washington DC. SFX created a miniature model which stood 1.8 m (5 ft) high, complete with miniature stairways, furniture, and pillars. Using forced perspective (placing the model a few metres away from the cameras so that it appears in the lens to be far away), nine cameras captured the explosion at high speed.

MAKING UP

One of the purposes of make-up in the movies is to make stars look glamorous despite hot studio lights. But even in the early black-and-white days, there was another demand – to make stars look hideous with features such as bloody scars and deep wrinkles. Films such as *Dr Jekyll and Mr Hyde* (1920) and *Frankenstein* (1931) created new monsters who terrified cinemagoers with their fanged teeth, blood-red eyes, and rotten flesh. Today, make-up experts use their skills in films such as *The Fly* (1986) to create weird and horrible creatures.

OPEN WOUND
When it comes to alien attacks, make-up artists have to create strange skin patterns and peculiar colours. This reptilian alien has been wounded by an arrow and is seeping green blood. The "blood" is created by mixing gelatine with food colouring until it is the right consistency.

BITING THE BULLET
Being bombarded with bullets in a western actually takes patience, planning, and plenty of red paint! Actors are fitted with plastic blood bags called squibs, which are put under their costumes and wired to tiny detonation charges. When the time comes, pyrotechnic experts behind the camera use remote control to set off these miniature explosions, which give the illusion of gunshot wounds without injuring the actor.

THE BLOOD BAG TREATMENT IN SAM PECKINPAH'S FILM *THE WILD BUNCH* (1969)

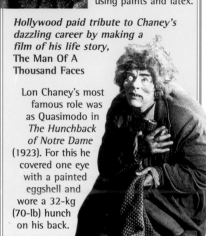

LON CHANEY
The first great master of horror make-up, Lon Chaney went to incredible lengths to portray deformed monsters and evil villains. The child of deaf-mute parents, he learned to express himself through facial expressions and became a star with his performances in *The Phantom of the Opera* (1925) and *The Unknown* (1927). He went to great lengths to deform his face using paints and latex.

Hollywood paid tribute to Chaney's dazzling career by making a film of his life story, The Man Of A Thousand Faces

Lon Chaney's most famous role was as Quasimodo in *The Hunchback of Notre Dame* (1923). For this he covered one eye with a painted eggshell and wore a 32-kg (70-lb) hunch on his back.

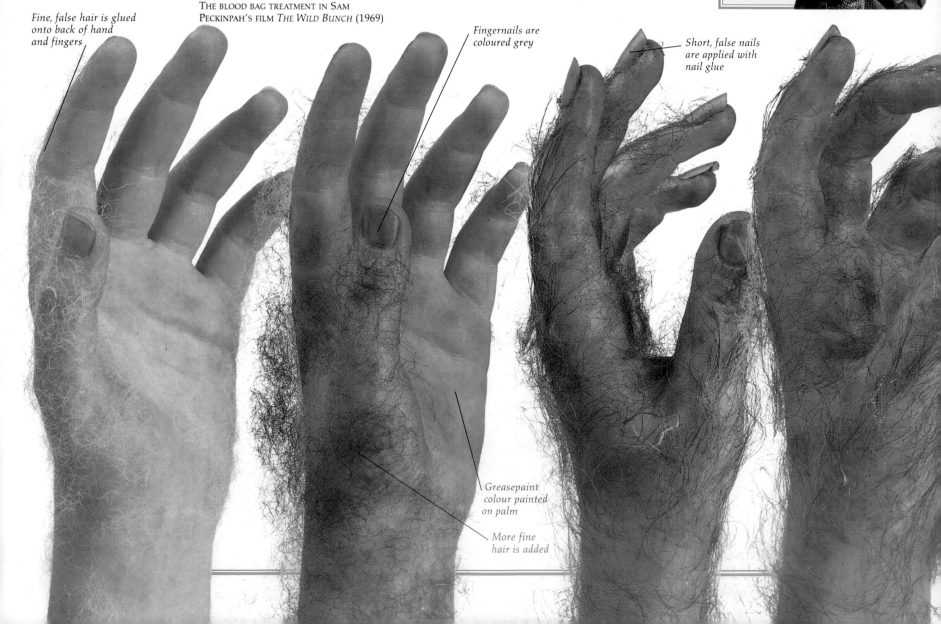

Fine, false hair is glued onto back of hand and fingers

Fingernails are coloured grey

Short, false nails are applied with nail glue

Greasepaint colour painted on palm

More fine hair is added

BRUSHES AND
GREASEPAINT

*Fake wrinkles and wispy
hair were added to make
Hoffman look old*

OLD HEAD ON
YOUNG SHOULDERS
In *Little Big Man* (1970),
Dustin Hoffman plays
121-year-old Jack Crabb,
a survivor of Custer's Last
Stand who remembers his
long life. Hoffman had to
suffer under a 14-piece
latex mask, which took
five hours a day to apply
under the hot lamps.

NYLON HAIR

LARGE
HAIR PIECE

REAL HAIR

FINE, FALSE HAIR ON FINE NET

THICK, FALSE
HAIR ON FINE NET

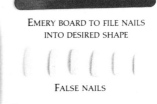

EMERY BOARD TO FILE NAILS
INTO DESIRED SHAPE

FALSE NAILS

GLUE TO ATTACH HAIR TO SKIN

A HOWLING SUCCESS
When it comes to werewolves,
the make-up experts in the
movie industry will bring out
the beast in anyone. In the
film *An American Werewolf
in London* (1981), make-up
expert Rick Baker won an
Oscar for his transformation
of actor David Naughton into
a claw-fingered beast. Here,
an actress's hand is changed by
the same process. Stop-motion
photography is used to capture
each stage of the gradual
alteration from normal
human being to werewolf.

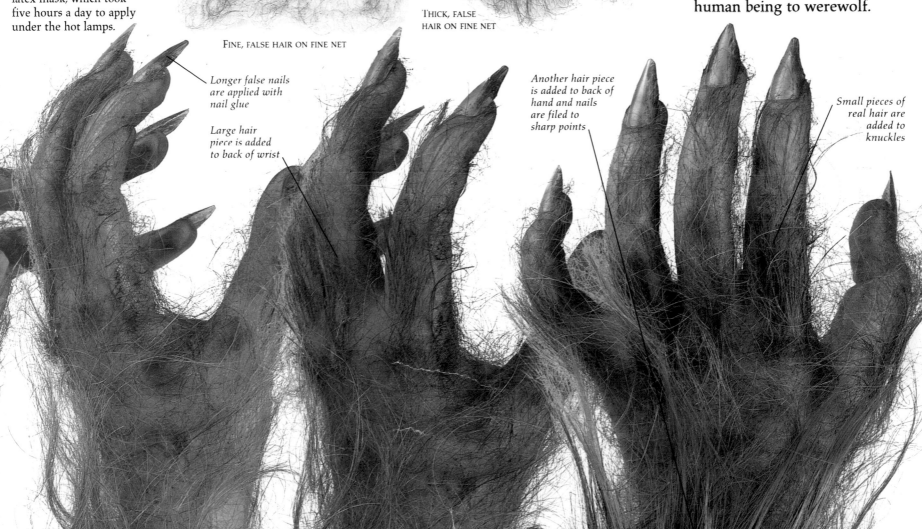

*Longer false nails
are applied with
nail glue*

*Large hair
piece is added
to back of wrist*

*Another hair piece
is added to back of
hand and nails
are filed to
sharp points*

*Small pieces of
real hair are
added to
knuckles*

A NEW IDENTITY

The make-up geniuses in the movie business can take the human face and body and transform it completely by means of a special effects process called prosthetics. With form-changing material such as foam latex, rubber, gelatine, and plaster, it is possible to completely change the physical appearance of an actor or actress, radically altering the shape of Jack Nicholson's mouth for The Joker in *Batman* (1989), or giving Robin Williams a whole new gender in *Mrs Doubtfire* (1993). The following pages demonstrate how prosthetics are custom-made and applied, transforming a mild-mannered model into a sinister alien.

The whole frightening costume was semi-transparent

Model's nose will not be changed

ALIEN BODY-BUILDING
To create the terrifying monster in *Alien* (1979), Oscar-winning artist H.R. Giger covered a 2.5 m (7 ft) tall actor in a full-body plaster cast. He then armed the plaster cast with false bones, Styrofoam, and a complex mixture of rubber and latex bases. The costume material was flexible and the huge head made of fibreglass so it could move quickly, like an insect's head.

MODEL FEATURES
Before the make-up artist applies any plaster, he must observe the actor's face and pick out which features need to be exaggerated in order to make the finished sculpture look as non-human as possible. In this case, the make-up artist decides to make use of the model's long face, creating prosthetics for the forehead, cheekbones, and the dome of the head.

Model's chin and mouth will not be altered by prosthetics for this make-up

Bald cap is shaped to fit round ears

The model stays perfectly still for ten minutes while the plaster sets

Container of medical adhesive

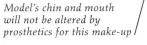

1 GETTING STARTED
The model is covered in protective clothing, and a bald rubber cap fitted over his head and hair. This is done so that the model's hair will not get moulded into the final prosthetic. For the perfect shape and cut, the make-up artist trims the bald cap around the ears and nape with scissors. He then sticks the edges of the cap to the model's head with an adhesive.

2 MOULDING THE HEAD
Strips of plaster scrim are dipped in water and moulded to the back of the head. These wet plaster strips are the same as those used in hospitals to protect broken bones and become very rigid. The back of the head is plastered because it is smooth and the plaster's edge will give the powdered alginate in stage 3 an edge to which to cling.

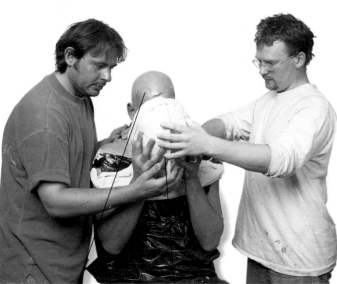

Two holes are left for the model to breathe through

Two make-up artists are needed because the alginate sets so quickly

3 FACEFUL OF CUSTARD

Powdered dental alginate is mixed with water to produce a custard-like mixture. This is applied over the model's face very quickly as it sets almost immediately. The alginate is smeared over the actor's closed mouth, closed eyes, ears, and nose, but the make-up artists leave two nasal holes clear so the model can still breathe! In just two minutes, the alginate is already beginning to set.

Dividing line between plaster and alginate

4 CUT IN HALF

From the side, it is possible to see how the plaster at the back of the head creates a boundary just behind the ears, with the setting alginate over the facial features. This boundary will later prove vital for the make-up artists, who use it to prise open the plaster cast.

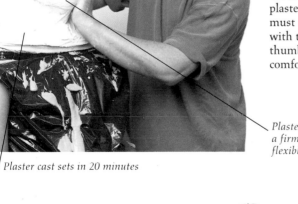

Plaster cast sets in 20 minutes

5 FINAL SET

When the algae has set, more plaster strips are added to cover the algae on the face and form a bridge with the plaster on the back of the head. The model's head is now fully wrapped up in plaster apart from two nose holes, and he must remain very calm. To communicate with the studio artists, he can give a thumbs up or down signal to express comfort or breathing difficulties.

Plaster is put on to make a firm support for the flexible alginate

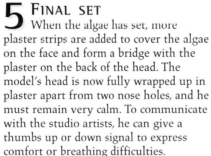

Model's eyes were closed throughout moulding process

Strong mould of head is made for next stage in creation of alien

Algae

Plaster

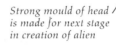

HOLLOW INSIDE OF CAST

FINAL CAST OF HEAD

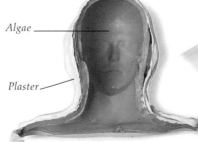

Bald cap still in position on head

Plaster cast is eased off face very carefully

6 LIFT OFF!

When the cast has become rigid, the technicians carefully cut the plaster cast across the top of the head, from ear to ear, lifting off the back of the cast first. Then the model scrunches his face up to release the mould while the technicians slowly ease the mask off forwards.

7 PERFECTLY CAST

Casting plaster, a fine gypsum powder mixed with water, is then poured into the hollow moulded head and left to dry. When this cast has set, the make-up artists are left with a perfect cast of the model's head. Now they can begin to model the alien features onto this cast.

Casting plaster being poured into hollow mould of head

Continued on next page...

8 CARVING IN CLAY

Using model drawings as a reference, the make-up artist uses clay to sculpt changes onto the mould of the model's head. He elongates and distorts the features of the face, especially the throat, cheekbones, forehead, and ears.

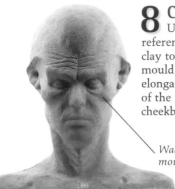

Wadges of clay are used to mould high cheekbones

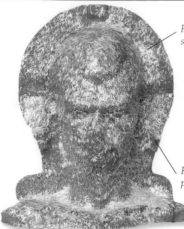

Fibreglass shreds

10 FINAL FIXING

Now the whole sculpture is covered with fibreglass matting, two layers on the flange and one on the rest of the head. Then the head is painted with another gel coat. The fibreglass is then left to go off (harden), and the mould split along the flange.

Flange across top of head marks place where mould will be split

Model-maker wears mask to protect against inhaling fibreglass

9 MAKING THE MOULD

The next stage is to make a fibreglass mould of the alien features. The mould will be split in half later to make the final prosthetic, so the model-maker creates a flange of clay across the head. He then covers the clay with a wax sealant and a gel coat of fibreglass resin. This is followed by a sprinkling of fibreglass shreds which will fill in detailed areas such as dips in the skin.

Prosthetic is painted by the make-up artist before it is applied to the model

Model's eyes are firmly shut when make-up is applied and talc applied immediately to prevent eye lashes sticking to anything!

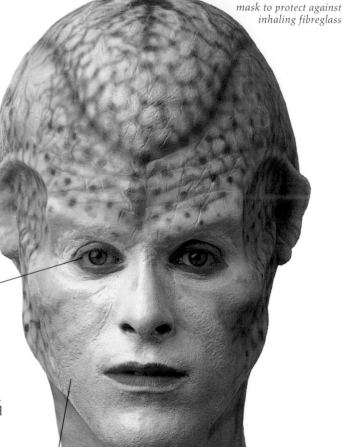

11 A PERFECT FIT

The original cast of the model's head (p. 35) is put inside the two pieces of fibreglass moulding which are sealed. Then prosthetic foam material is poured between the cast head and the larger mould, filling the spaces where the model-maker sculpted changes in clay. The resulting prosthetic is painted and placed on the model's head (left), so the make-up process can begin.

Halfway through, the edges of the prosthetic have been completely blended in with make-up

---

BIRTH OF AN ALIEN

1 Make-up artists have to be careful when fixing a mask to an actor's face – the foam edges around the eyes, nose, and mouth are delicate and easily torn. The mask is fitted to the face and neck using a medical spirit-based adhesive.

2 Getting an actor into a prosthetic mask can be tricky. The mask has a large slit down the centre of the back that allows the actor to slip into it. The edges of the slit are glued down, and disguised with clever make-up.

3 Whenever the artist applies make-up to the model's face, he dabs on talc. The talc stops the very strong adhesive sticking to anything that it comes in contact with.

Artist's air-brush

4 The make-up artist gives the alien skin as much character as possible. Over the acrylic artist's ink mixed with adhesive that is used as a base colour, he air-brushes in details such as the veining on the head.

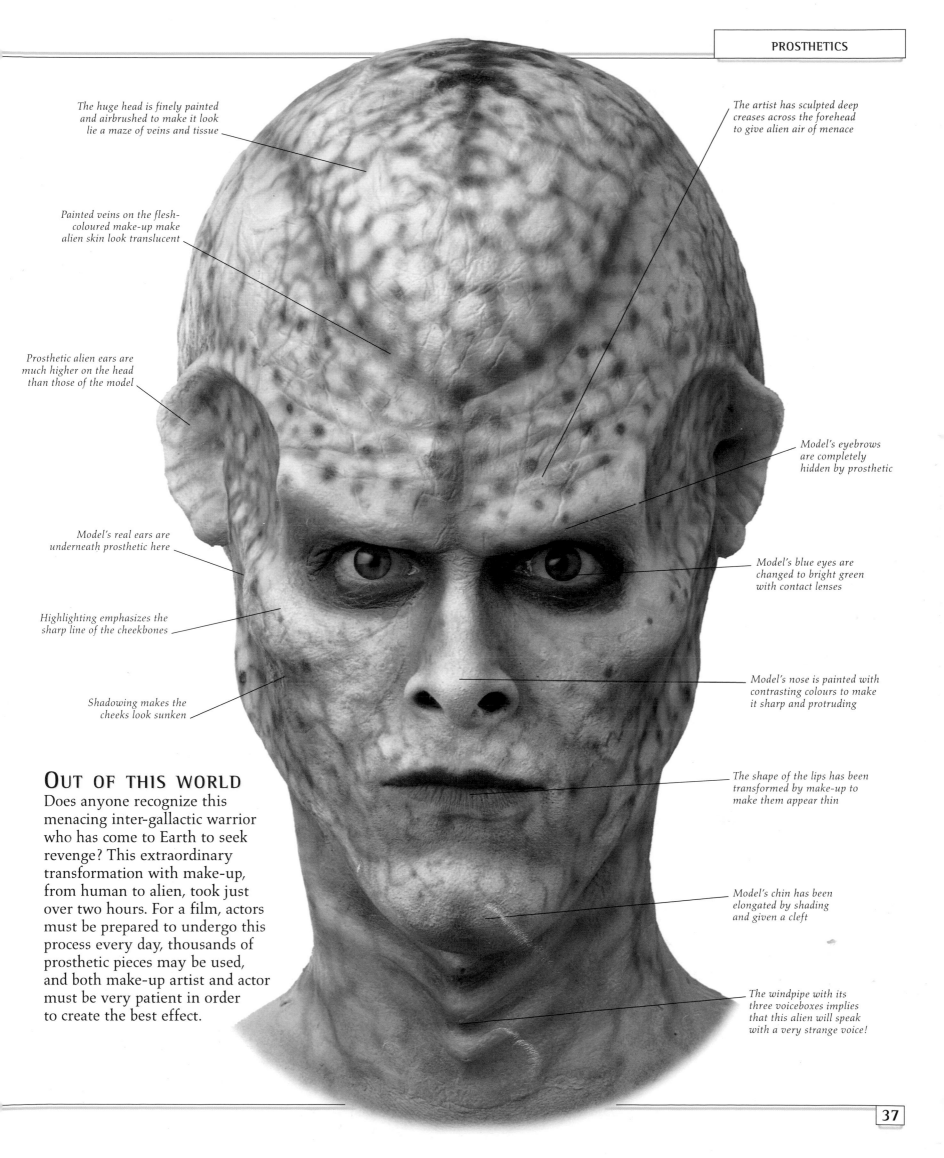

The huge head is finely painted and airbrushed to make it look lie a maze of veins and tissue

The artist has sculpted deep creases across the forehead to give alien air of menace

Painted veins on the flesh-coloured make-up make alien skin look translucent

Prosthetic alien ears are much higher on the head than those of the model

Model's eyebrows are completely hidden by prosthetic

Model's real ears are underneath prosthetic here

Model's blue eyes are changed to bright green with contact lenses

Highlighting emphasizes the sharp line of the cheekbones

Model's nose is painted with contrasting colours to make it sharp and protruding

Shadowing makes the cheeks look sunken

OUT OF THIS WORLD

Does anyone recognize this menacing inter-gallactic warrior who has come to Earth to seek revenge? This extraordinary transformation with make-up, from human to alien, took just over two hours. For a film, actors must be prepared to undergo this process every day, thousands of prosthetic pieces may be used, and both make-up artist and actor must be very patient in order to create the best effect.

The shape of the lips has been transformed by make-up to make them appear thin

Model's chin has been elongated by shading and given a cleft

The windpipe with its three voiceboxes implies that this alien will speak with a very strange voice!

TAKING FLIGHT

Batman may fly through the air with the greatest of ease,
but getting him to stay there can prove a difficult job for the
SFX team. Superheroes and flying creatures are usually connected to a
special flying rig, complete with safety wires and pulley systems operated by
technicians. Blue-screen backgrounds that can be replaced by, for example,
cloudy skylines or starry deep space, are used to give the illusion of flight.
Stuntpeople also use flying rigs to control falls when they are leaping
from tall buildings and high mountains. It may look like terrific action
on screen, but falling through the sky requires plenty of groundwork!

Motorcycle disc brakes are used for emergency stops

Fan blades rotate at a constant speed

Cable runs from thick to thin end of tapered cone

Steel supporting cable 4mm (³⁄₁₆ in) thick

Harness is anchored at centre of front or centre of back

Fan descender is screwed to scaffolding at these points

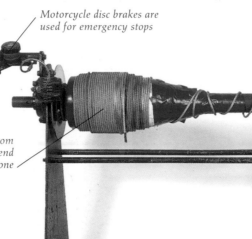

HARNESS USED WITH FAN DESCENDER

FAN DESCENDER USED FOR A CONTROLLED FALL

CONTROLLING THE DESCENT

A fan descender is used for many falling stunts.
A cable runs from the fan descender and is
attached to a harness on the stuntperson (left).
The fan itself turns at a constant speed. However,
the 6mm (¼ in) cable is arranged on a cone-
shaped rotating holder and moves from the
thicker end to the thinner end of the cone.
This slows the descent of the person falling.

Fan descender controls the fall

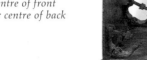

Any wires not hidden by the flurry of fake snow will be eliminated in post production

CLIFF FALL

In the film *Cliffhanger* (1993), Sylvester Stallone
has to contend with a group of ruthless killers on
treacherous mountain terrain. Stuntpeople were
called in for the many spectacular cliff falls used in
the film as Stallone tries to escape his enemies. For
this scene, a stuntman appeared to fall from a snowy
clifftop in a studio set-up. Under his outer clothing
he is wearing a climbing harness that is attached to
a fan descender operated by the men top right.

Rig is weighted for greater control by special effects supervisor

Supporting beam

Cable runs through pulleys to technician controlling the rig

The rig can take 239 kg (525 lb) breaking strain on the wires

T-bar carries thin wires that support actor

THE FLYING RIG

In his many films, Superman soars like an eagle, but he would not get far without a flying rig. The flying rig operates as a simple pulley system. The actor is strapped into a hip-hugging flying harness, which in turn is connected to very thin wires on a steel T-bar. The T-bar is supported by galvanized steel cable which runs through a series of pulleys. The cabling is used once only for a film, and then replaced, for strict safety reasons.

MISSION ACCOMPLISHED

When the character played by Tom Cruise has to infiltrate a top secret base to steal an all-important computer chip in *Mission Impossible* (1996), he uses a flying rig on screen to fool the intricate alarm system. The floors and walls of the room in the film are sensitive to the touch, and the rig is used to hover the actor just centimetres above the ground. Cruise was attached to the pulley system, and the harness was adjusted to his weight so that he would not spin in the air.

TOM CRUISE RISKING EVERYTHING IN *MISSION IMPOSSIBLE*

The wires are just 1.5mm thick so they can be digitally erased for the film

Harness is normally hidden under the actor's clothing

Instead of being hidden, a flying harness becomes an important prop

Child wearing flying harness

Turbulence caused by suction of hover mower

Balance of harness can be adjusted to allow for actor's long legs or torso

Leather straps fasten round hips and legs

© Disney

FLYING HARNESS

HOVER MOWER FROM HELL

When an eccentric inventor, played by Rick Moranis, accidentally shrinks his children to the size of ants in *Honey, I Shrunk the Kids* (1989), the children have to travel across their garden to get home. They avoid various dangers in their journey, including being sucked up by a giant hover mower. In this studio shot, one child is being hauled upwards towards the mower on a flying rig, while the others run for cover.

CRASH LANDING

The most dangerous job in the movie business has always been that of the stuntperson. As stunt double to an actor or actress, they may be called upon to leap from the top of a waterfall, jump from a helicopter, or be thrown through the air by a mighty explosion. Of course, these action sequences are great fun to watch, but they require the utmost attention to safety and planning in order to succeed without killing anyone. Films such as *Raiders of the Lost Ark* (1981), *Die Hard* (1988), and *Midnight Run* (1991) have all used spectacular stunts to make their films more exciting and appealing to an ever more demanding audience. By using carefully rigged devices such as air rams, clever substitutes such as sugar glass, and hidden padded clothing, stuntpeople live to make another film.

AIR RAM

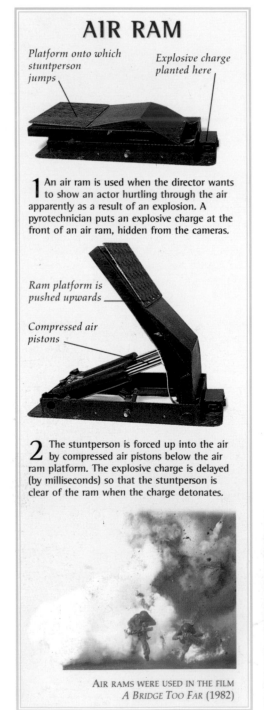

Platform onto which stuntperson jumps

Explosive charge planted here

1 An air ram is used when the director wants to show an actor hurtling through the air apparently as a result of an explosion. A pyrotechnician puts an explosive charge at the front of an air ram, hidden from the cameras.

Ram platform is pushed upwards

Compressed air pistons

2 The stuntperson is forced up into the air by compressed air pistons below the air ram platform. The explosive charge is delayed (by milliseconds) so that the stuntperson is clear of the ram when the charge detonates.

AIR RAMS WERE USED IN THE FILM
A BRIDGE TOO FAR (1982)

LETHAL CRUNCH

The explosive finale to *Lethal Weapon* (1987) shows policeman Mel Gibson chasing his enemies through the busy evening rush-hour traffic of the city of Los Angeles. When an oncoming bus hurtles into a passing car, there is a huge crash. This stunt was co-ordinated to perfection, with every detail and issue of safety – from the speed of the bus to the position of the car – rehearsed over and over again, until the director finally let the cameras roll.

SAFETY CLOTHING

When stuntpeople jump off moving trains, get thrown from speeding cars, or leap off tall buildings, they are always protected with padded suits to prevent injury on landing. They must also know exactly how to land to prevent breaking bones, and their back, arms, and shoulders are usually well padded to break the fall. On screen, their outer clothing hides the streamlined padding.

The lightweight car is positioned to the left of the oncoming bus for maximum impact

Attention to detail by the modelmaker makes this scene very convincing

CRUISING OUT OF CONTROL

Big-budget explosions do not always have to be undertaken with huge sets and detailed preparation. For the film *Speed 2: Cruise Control* (1997), a luxury boat sails head-on into a tourist resort causing widespread destruction and chaos. The filmmakers decided to use a miniature model for the climactic scene, making sure that the hotels, beach houses, and luxury boat looked completely life-like. Tiny explosives were inserted into the models.

Padded suit protects shoulder and upper body and is used for jumps from a height

Torso padding is laced on to protect the stomach and lower back during falls

The back can be protected by this spinal padding

LEAP OF FAITH

James Bond must always be prepared to jump through a window or fall off a charging tank to evade capture. In *Goldeneye* (1995), agent 007 leaps from a huge glass window to escape his killers. The stunt was performed by Pierce Brosnan's stunt double, who was kitted out in protective clothing and padding. The glass he falls through is sugar glass, which will not cut him. There is a soft mattress out of shot to break his fall, and the jump is timed to give the camera crew the best angles. As always with stunts, the action is meticulously planned and tested in advance.

When the bus hits, an explosive beneath the car's chassis is set off

The bus driver is actually a stuntman strapped safely into his seat to prevent injury during the big crunch

FIRE! FIRE!

Huge fires have been created for many films from *Gone With the Wind* (1939) to *Always* (1989), and many others involve much smaller, but no less complicated, fire scenes. Whenever fire is involved, the pyrotechnician creates a safety zone, which only he or she crosses in order to set fuses, to spray flammable liquid, or to wire detonators. Stuntmen or women take the place of actors and actresses for the more dangerous scenes involving fire, particularly when someone is to be set alight, or is to be filmed escaping from the heart of an inferno. Special clothing and gels are used, and all fires are carefully controlled.

Gel lowers body temperature so much that it can only be in contact with skin for a maximum of 30 minutes

FIRE RETARDANT GEL

Thin Nomex suit is soaked in fire retardant gel before the stuntperson puts it on

Stuntperson breathes in oxygen through mouthpiece

RAGING INFERNO
The film *Backdraft* (1991) follows the great tradition of epic fire films established by *Towering Inferno* (1974), by using actual fireballs and flames on set with the actors. Director Ron Howard made sure that the pyrotechnics were tightly controlled and everyone was kept at a safe distance while actors Kurt Russell and Robert De Niro surged through the flames. CGi fire images were also added later to increase the drama.

PUTTING IT OUT
On every set where fire is to play a part, there have to be fire extinguishers and safety officers present. Strict safety procedures are followed to avoid injury to people or unplanned damage to sets.

BREATHING IN
If a scene requires someone to remain in a smoky atmosphere for any length of time, he or she needs to wear an oxygen mask to breathe properly. The small oxygen tank (above) can be easily concealed under clothing.

CREATING A FLAME
Flame effects are created and destroyed by trained pyrotechnicians skilled in safely manipulating specialist equipment such as flame forks and flame drums. To create the flames that frame this page, a device known as a fire bar (above), was used. The fire bar is fuelled by gas, and the amount of gas being fed in controls the height of the flames.

Gas escapes through holes along the surface of the fire bar

NOMEX SUIT

Rainsuit worn to keep fire retardant in, insulating it so it cannot evaporate

RAINSUIT

RACING DRIVER'S SUIT

FIRE RETARDANT PROSTHETIC MASK

Stuntman is protected by fire retardant gel under clothing

Sometimes a suit like those worn by racing drivers is worn over the rainsuit

Racing driver gloves may be worn

FIRE RETARDANT PROSTHETIC HANDS

HOT UNDER THE COLLAR

When close-ups are needed that involve someone being set on fire, the stuntperson must use a special prosthetic mask so that they appear to be the actor wrapped in flames. Stuntman Sean McCabe is seen here wearing fireproof clothing, together with a prosthetic head and hands. The mask is fire retardant and has a special tube from the mouth round which he clamps his teeth to seal the mask. After a maximum of only 20 seconds, the flames must be put out, because that is as long as he is able to hold his breath.

FIRE PROTECTION

Running through an inferno of smoke and fire is one of the most dangerous stunts, and the stuntperson must be fully protected before doing a fire scene. A special Nomex suit is soaked in ice-cold fire retardant gel that lowers the body· temperature, so providing resistance for a short period to the heat of the flames. A racing suit can be put on next for extra protection, and a costume is worn over everything, daubed in flammable liquid, and set alight.

EXPLOSIVE ACTION

Creating explosive effects for the screen usually involves a high level of danger, so it is necessary for a film crew to take great safety precautions to avoid disaster. The pyrotechnic expert is perhaps the most safety-conscious person working on a film set. To rig huge explosions involving gunpowder, diesel, and propane, while making sure that the entire film crew is safe, is an exacting task. On top of this, many explosions can only be set up once, and the timing must work perfectly. Most special effects are fired with electronic fuses so that each blast is timed with split-second accuracy from a safe distance, particularly when the effect involves stuntpeople or actors.

DYING HARD
One of the hair-raising scenes in *Die Hard 2* (1990) involves Detective John McClane (Bruce Willis) in ejecting himself from the cockpit of an exploding plane. Willis was first filmed in front of a blue screen while strapped to an ejection-seat rig in the studio. The actual fireball explosion was filmed on location using a mock-up plane and a fire-resistant overhead camera.

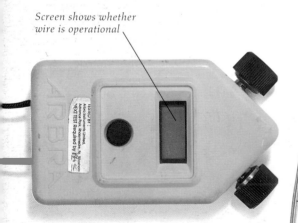

STUNTMEN FLY THROUGH THE AIR IN *BLOWN AWAY* (1994)

PLANNING A STUNT
Although many explosions look haphazard and destructive on screen, the planning and preparation of these scenes is extremely detailed and planned to the last second. Experts use specific explosives in order to produce the desired blast within a designated area. Stuntmen wear protective clothing (pp. 40–41) and are strategically positioned when the explosion goes off so that they are safe from permanent harm.

TITANIUM POWDER

BOMB

GUNPOWDER

GOING LIKE A BOMB
Pyrotechnic experts want every explosion to be unique. To achieve this, they create special mixes to produce different kinds of explosions. The explosion of this model car (right) was created with small "bombs" made with a combination of gunpowder and titanium. The "bombs" are fused and wired up to a firebox, which is used to detonate the explosions.

Screen shows whether wire is operational

Fuse wire leading to charge

Numbered buttons for manual control

Terminal

Battery lead

Dial for firing all charges simultaneously

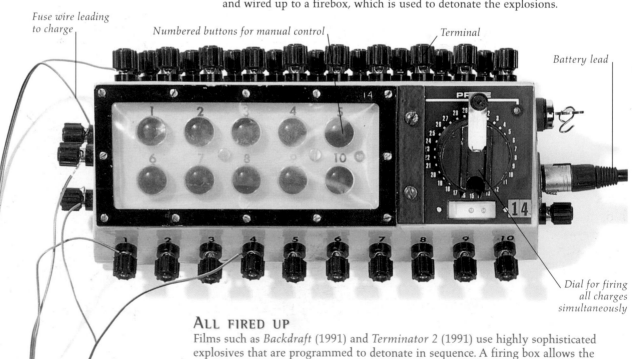

A TESTING TIME
It only takes one mistake for thousands of dollars to be wasted on a film shoot. To avoid problems of this sort in pyrotechnics, everything is checked rigorously before any attempt is made to set off an explosion. The director will use several high speed cameras to capture a blast. Pyrotechnicians use an electronic testing box to check that every wire leading from the explosive to the detonator is operational.

ALL FIRED UP
Films such as *Backdraft* (1991) and *Terminator 2* (1991) use highly sophisticated explosives that are programmed to detonate in sequence. A firing box allows the pyrotechnician to operate at a safe distance but have perfect control over any sequence of explosions. Each explosive is wired to a different terminal, and these can be set to go off in order automatically, or the buttons can be punched by the pyrotechnician.

*Placing of bombs
ensures a fireball
without too much smoke*

*An explosive charge
was taped to the
door of the car*

MODEL BLAST

Cars are forever being
blown to pieces in films,
but pyrotechnicians must
make sure that the blast does
not smother the car and cloud
the camera's view of the explosion
with smoke. To blow up this model
car, two small "bombs" were placed
behind the car doors, while a larger
one was placed beneath the chassis. The
bombs were wired to the firing box, and
the film crew stood behind a safety line.

BATTLE ZONE

Capturing action scenes on camera often means turning the film set into a battle zone. Films such as *Platoon* (1986), *Dances With Wolves* (1990), and *The Last of the Mohicans* (1992) feature large-scale battle scenes with mortar bombs, explosives, and gunfire surrounding the actors as they do battle. Such sequences require detailed planning and preparation to achieve spectacular effects. It can look like complete bedlam on screen, and pyrotechnicians have to ensure that explosions are precisely timed, and that actors are at a safe distance from devices such as mortars when they are exploded.

CORK ROCKS

PEAT

VERMICULITE

EXPLODING ONTO THE SCENE

When houses and buildings explode in the movies, they usually create widespread destruction and chaos. Filming these nail-biting scenes requires a high degree of preparation and attention to safety. For this scene in *Last Action Hero* (1993), explosives were placed near the windows, doors, and on the roof to give maximum impact, without damage spreading too far.

Gun has a trigger and barrel, and is fired exactly like a real firearm

Shoulder stock

Hose supplies air from compressor or cylinder

Gauges show air pressure

GAS GUN

Actors never use real guns during battle sequences – they are too dangerous to handle and could cause serious injury. Instead, special effects technicians have developed special "cinema" guns which simulate gunfire with absolute safety. This compressed air gun (above) looks exactly like the real thing, but fires only soft gelatin pellets. Filled with fake blood, and fired at an actor's body, the soft pellets burst, giving the same grisly effect as a bullet wound.

The taller and thinner the mortar, the higher the debris travels

MORTAR

Debris from mortars flies high into the air

Arnold Schwarzenegger holds his own in True Lies

A HAIL OF BULLETS

Scenes such as this one from *True Lies* (1994) show actors dodging a hail of bullets. To look convincing, special effects technicians often use compressed air guns to fire pellets into the walls, floor, and ceiling. They also set charges into the plaster of, for example, a wall, and detonate them one by one in sequence to give the impression that someone is spraying bullets round the room. Computer generated bullet holes are also added to prevent actors coming to harm.

AMERICAN CIVIL WAR FILM *GLORY* (1989)

CHARGING INTO BATTLE

In war films, directors often want to show battlefield scenes with men charging through open spaces surrounded by explosions and showered with debris. To do this, the special effects team digs metal containers called mortars (right) into the ground to create explosions at the touch of a button. The position of the mortars are plainly marked on the ground so that the actors can avoid running directly over them, and the effects staff set them off electronically.

WHAT A BLAST!

Mortars are packed with different mixtures to give different effects. They can contain peat, vermiculite (builder's dust), and lumps of cork that look like clods of earth when they fly through the air. Rubber dust can be added to make it all look blacker. There are different shapes of mortar as well. If a mortar is shallow with a wide top, the explosion will travel outwards over a wide area.

SMOKE CARTRIDGE

GROUNDBURST SIMULATOR

Fuse wire connects to detonator

STUDIO FLASHPOT

IGNITER CORD

SMOKE

There are all kinds of devices in the pyrotechnician's bag of tricks. They can not only create fire without smoke, but smoke without fire. When lit, fast igniter cord fizzes and lights up the scene, and a studio flashpot produces a mushroom cloud with a flash and sparks. Smoke cartridges come in all sizes, and the smaller ones are used in the studio. For large outdoor explosions, such as this one created for *A Bridge Too Far* (1982), pyrotechnicians use gas jet explosives and large smoke cartridges. While the gas jet explosives provide the bang and throw out debris, the smoke cartridges produce huge, dense clouds of smoke.

SNOW AND ICE

SFX technicians can create snowstorms, blizzards, avalanches, and glaciers in the safe surroundings of a film studio. Instead of having to travel to the wintry landscapes of the Siberian Arctic or the Swiss Alps, film magicians can recreate harsh conditions with miniature sets, snow machines, fake frost, and icicles. Some films, such as *The Empire Strikes Back* (1980), use real footage of snowy locations and later add special effects blizzards in the studio. Others, such as *Goldeneye* (1995), use miniature snow mountains and computer-generated avalanches without setting foot outside the studio door. These snow and ice effects have many benefits. Studio technicians can actually control the force and speed of the snowstorms. They can also save money and prevent the actor or actress from coming to any harm.

It is difficult to hold your ground against the wind machine

A FROZEN WINTER

Much of the epic *Doctor Zhivago* (1965), directed by the legendary director David Lean, is set in the winter. Canada was used as a location for the frozen Russian countryside. Lean used tonnes of artificial snow and frost in his elaborate set designs. To create a frosted windowpane (right), artificial frost is sprayed onto the glass and then brightly lit by studio lights. Icicles (above) are made from plastic that is formed as cones on heated moulds.

OMAR SHARIF IN *DOCTOR ZHIVAGO*

Salt clings easily to surfaces such as roofs

BUMBLE THE BEADLE TRYING TO SELL OLIVER IN *OLIVER!*

Large salt crystals give the appearance and crunch underfoot of real snow

THE STREETS OF LONDON

When Lionel Bart's hit musical *Oliver!* (1969) was turned into a big-budget film, director Carol Reed wanted to create the harsh atmosphere of Victorian London in which the young orphan has to survive. To portray the bitter cold of the snowy city, the production crew covered an entire alley with dendritic salt, a special salt which has large crystals. The camera was fitted with a fog filter to give the location a cold and chilly feeling.

BLOWN AWAY

Seen through a frosted window covered with icicles a frozen child battles her way through a tremendous snow blizzard. In reality, this scene was created in the confines of a warm film studio. The snow on the ground and across the window ledge at the bottom of the picture is salt, while the hanging icicles were moulded from plastic.

Salt sticks to water sprayed on clothing

Salt "snow" on window ledge

TONNES AND TONNES OF SNOW

The whole plot of *Die Hard 2* takes place during a massive snowstorm. When snowbound locations proved difficult to find, the crew decided to use a disused airport and special effects snowflakes. In the final scene, when Detective John McClane (Bruce Willis) confronts the terrorists, over 45,500 kg (100,000 lb) of plastic flakes were used for ground snow, while huge ice crushers were trucked in to make giant mounds of ice. Bruce Willis was then blasted by snow machines.

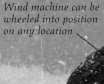

BRUCE WILLIS IN *DIE HARD 2* (1990)

Windowframe held in position by clamps

Technician cranking handle for extra snow

Technician throwing snow into back

Technician operating smoke machine

"Snow" piled high in hand-operated feeder

THE WHOLE PICTURE

Although we see only the snowstorm and child through the windowpane, the entire studio effect is much more complicated. Two bright umbrella lights bounce off the purple background on either side of the set, while a technician crouches over a smoke machine in the foreground. The smoke, made by mixing glycerine and water, gives a misty effect. Another technician operates the wind machine and shovels plastic or paper "snow" through the wind blades.

Cranking handle to drop more snow into blast of air

Wind machine is a giant fan that pushes the air and snow through

Artificial snow is blown out of front of machine

BLOWING UP A STORM

It is possible to create really violent weather effects in the studio with a simple wind machine. Tiny white plastic or paper shreds are thrown into the back of the machine, sucked through and blown out the front. The wind machine is connected to a variable voltage system which can alter the speed and power of its blades, while a hand-operated feeder can also be used to add to the effect.

Wind machine can be wheeled into position on any location

Voltage control alters speed of wind machine

NATURAL DISASTERS

A building rips apart when struck by lightning, a battered car floats down the high street in a torrential flood, tractors fall from the skies during a spectacular tornado. These are just a few of the many breathtaking set pieces conjured up by special effects experts to show the destructive power of the world's natural disasters. Miniature models (pp. 28–31), full-scale explosions (pp. 44–45), and matte paintings (pp. 16–17) have all been used in films to portray the effects of violent storms, destructive earthquakes, and erupting volcanoes. For a local effect, wind machines and rain heads are employed (pp. 48–49). For extreme effect, recent films such as *Twister* (1996) and *Dante's Peak* (1997) have used CGi (pp. 54–57) to visualize the dark side of nature in all its terrifying glory.

TERRIFYING TORNADOES

Tornadoes have been made for films in various mechanical ways, including the use of fog machines, but for the film *Twister* (1996) the latest in computer-generated technology brought the power of the dark side of nature to the screen. Using a combination of real weather footage shot in Tornado Alley, Texas, and some revolutionary CGi, the film captures the terror of such high winds. The digital twisters were added to real footage, filmed months in advance, of actors running for cover.

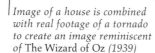

Image of a house is combined with real footage of a tornado to create an image reminiscent of The Wizard of Oz *(1939)*

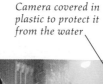

Camera covered in plastic to protect it from the water

CGi flame adds drama to the scene

LOS ANGELES STREETS AWASH IN LAVA IN *VOLCANO*

FLOODED!

Filming the action scenes in huge water tanks for the disaster film *Hard Rain* (1998) was a soggy business. All the filming equipment on set, from the boom microphones to the camera cranes, had to be covered in plastic to prevent damage from the large quantities of water used. In turn, the actors were playing their roles up to their necks in water, and special safety teams were kept on stand-by to watch out for them.

UP TO THEIR NECKS IN WATER ON THE SET OF *HARD RAIN*

IN THE HOT SPOT

Hollywood, California, is one of the hottest places in the United States, but in the film *Volcano* (1997), the temperature soars through the roof! An underground volcano engulfs the city of Los Angeles in lava, turning it into a molten mass. Using both miniature models and full-scale buildings, the crew filmed the destruction of Los Angeles streets, later adding huge lava rivers with the aid of digital technology.

Film of real twisters provides the dramatic basis for film footage

FRIGHTENING LIGHTNING

Lightning is virtually impossible to capture on a film shoot. Instead, filmmakers have learned to rely on storm effects generated on the computer. Forked lightning can be created and manipulated on screen and the accompanying thunder claps reproduced in a sound studio. Films such as *Ghostbusters* (1984), *Cape Fear* (1991), and *Jurassic Park* (1993) and have used computer techniques to good effect, producing spectacular and unforgettable storms on screen.

Computerized lightning is combined with real film footage

CGI ELEMENTS LET RIP IN *GHOSTBUSTERS*

Harrison Ford wrestles with the raft in turbulent waters

CREATING A STORM AT SEA

Filming disaster scenes on location is a complicated affair. It is sometimes necessary to move actors, crew, and equipment right around the world, and this can cause problems. For the climax to the film *Mosquito Coast* (1986), Harrison Ford and his screen family have to face a destructive monsoon storm as they float downriver on a makeshift raft. Filming with waterproofed equipment – and wearing waterproofs or diving suits themselves – in what were actually calm conditions at sea, the special effects team created a chaotic scene in stormy waters.

FINISHED SCENE FROM *THE MOSQUITO COAST*

Film crew revs boat's engine to create turbulence in the water

Huge wind machines (pp. 48–49) are used

Waterproofed cameras capture close-ups

Soundman has to get close to the actors

WATER EFFECTS

From raging rivers to light drizzle, getting water to behave itself on camera can be a slippery job. Battleships and boats are relatively easy to film as they float on the water's surface, but diving down into the murky depths of the ocean demands the very best in special effects wizardry. Most of *20,000 Leagues Under the Sea* (1997) was filmed in the Pacific Ocean, with the crew wearing diving gear and using special watertight filming equipment. Other films, such as *Jaws* (1975), used huge, glass-sided water tanks to film complex action sequences that could not be achieved in the sea because of the unpredictability of tide and weather. And, when it comes to storms at sea, submarine battles or giant octopus attacks, technicians create fantastic sub-aqua worlds in the studio without water!

FILMING IN A DELUGE
In Sylvester Stallone's *Cliffhanger* (1993) a camera crane towers above a rescue helicopter while giant rain stands spray water over the actors. The camera and studio lights have been covered with waterproof sheets in order to protect them from the damp, and water is piped across the ground in a continuous flow.

LOOK, NO WHEELS!
For complicated underwater shots, deep-sea photographers use special cameras to film under the sea. In *The Spy Who Loved Me*, a life-size model of James Bond's Lotus car was left buoyant in the water while ace cameraman Mike Valentine filmed the getaway with an underwater Arriflex camera (pp. 12–13).

SUBMARINE IN A FOG
You do not have to travel to the bottom of the ocean to create a convincing shot of a submarine travelling underwater. You do not even have to use water! This miniature set of a sea canyon, scaled to the correct size for the model submarine that has to travel through it, was built and painted in the studio by special effects technicians in only two days. For many films, such shots can take months of preparation.

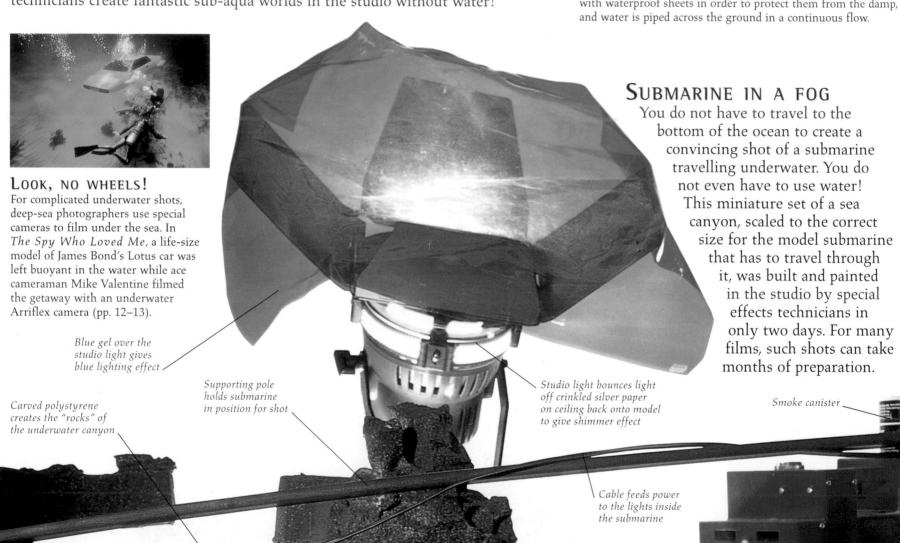

Blue gel over the studio light gives blue lighting effect

Supporting pole holds submarine in position for shot

Studio light bounces light off crinkled silver paper on ceiling back onto model to give shimmer effect

Smoke canister

Carved polystyrene creates the "rocks" of the underwater canyon

Cable feeds power to the lights inside the submarine

Rain head is directional and the pressure can be altered to change the falling water from a shower to a downpour

Powerful studio lights shine light onto the plain background to increase the visibility of the rain

Large drops of "rain" water become visible against boy's clothing

Pump sends water from water trough up through pipe to rain head

Water collects in water trough at base

Smoke is made by mixing water and glycerine

Technician controls amount of smoke being emitted

RAIN RAIN GO AWAY!

Water, like fire, has to be filmed full-size as it cannot be scaled down. This studio shot of a rain-soaked boy with an umbrella uses the same technique as was used for Gene Kelly's legendary dance sequence in *Singin' in the Rain* (1952). A specially designed rain head sprinkles water from above and two powerful studio lights enhance the visibility of the water droplets.

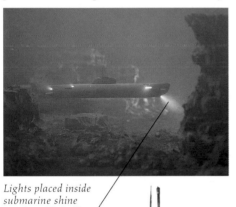

Lights placed inside submarine shine out for added effect

Model submarine clamped in position

Flock – a model-makers' scenic material – is used to give texture to the scenery

NOT A DROP OF WATER

The submarine cruises over the ocean floor on a top secret mission. The right combination of smoke machine, light reflectors, miniature set, and model have created a startlingly realistic illusion. Films such as *The Hunt for Red October* (1990) and *The Abyss* (1989) used the same techniques in the studio for action sequences – models moving in smoke, with coloured lighting from above.

SMOKE IN THE STUDIO

To make the miniature scene as realistic as possible, technicians must control the amount of smoke filling the set. Too little smoke will mean the studio background will show, while too much smoke will cloud the model submarine. To create the right texture, only small bursts of smoke are used.

Matte emulsion paint gives that realistic rocky look to the polystyrene

Expanding filler foam gives the "rocks" a bumpy surface

DIGITAL DRAGONS

Computer special effects have changed the look of cinema forever. Instead of creating models of dinosaurs and space creatures in the studio, cutting-edge technology can create these three-dimensional images on a computer, making them look as realistic as the actors with whom they share the screen. From the eye-popping T-rex attack in *Jurassic Park* (1993) to the gently floating feather in *Forrest Gump* (1994), computer-generated images – CGi – now dominate every aspect of modern filmmaking. New techniques such as motion capture, pixel-stretching, morphing and wire-framing are extending the frontiers of CGi by the day, taking the cinema-goer into a whole new world of big screen magic.

Special attention was given to Draco's face, which was given the same facial expressions as Sean Connery, who supplied the voiceover

Wings must be constructed with different wire frames to show them stretched out wide in flight or tucked into body

"Viewpaint" software technology allows the operator to paint spines and scales on the dragon's body

DRACO THE DRAGON

In the film *Dragonheart* (1997) a dragon-slaying knight teams up with the last of the dragons to battle an evil ruler. To make the fire-breathing creature look realistic, special effects technicians scanned a 1.5 m (4 ft) model into a computer and then constructed a virtual dragon on screen. Digital computer wizardry was used to make Draco the dragon breathe fire, as well as talk and interact with the actors in the film.

COMPUTERIZED MONSTERS

Creating a dragon on the computer involves intensive research and painstaking attention to detail. First, a three-dimensional image, called a "wire frame", is created on screen. This is done by using specific digital lines connected to key parts of the dragon's body to form a digital skeleton. Then a special software program is used to mould the dragon's muscles, which will make it appear to move realistically, around the frame. Finally, "Viewpaint" technology is used to paint the dragon on screen, giving it the computer-generated skin, bone, and flesh of a living, breathing creature.

Wire frame is built up in stages, animators giving life to the data by moving the measurements frame by frame

Dragon's tail can be enlarged or decreased in size by stretching the lines and body points of the wire frame

To make the dragon stand upright on its haunches, the computer experts measure the feet and legs against the body to give the correct height reading

Digital measurements must be exact and in scale with the whole image

Background footage is filmed months in advance, and is then combined with the computer generated dragon in the final film

The dragon's eyes are modelled on those of a lizard, and are digitally created using special software to make them blink, move, and close shut

The dragon's mouth and snout will be digitally animated to show facial expressions and breath CGi fire

Skin textures, shadows and body armour are all painted on the wire-frame dragon as if painting a 3-D model

COMPUTER MAGIC

With the dawn of computer generated images – CGi – the film world has taken great leaps into the unknown. Films such as *Terminator 2* and *The Abyss* have paved the way for some of the most dazzling special effects ever seen on the screen. With each passing year, another film comes along to break the mould in computer generated wizardry. *Dragonheart* (pp. 54–55), *Ghost*, and *The Mask* have all used ground-breaking digital techniques such as wire-framing, pixel-stretching, and morphing to reproduce in turn talking, dragons breathing fire, ghosts that walk through walls, and outrageous green-faced pranksters.

TWISTED
The physical mishaps of the character played by Meryl Streep in *Death Becomes Her* (1992) walk a fine line between the fantastical and downright painful! For the famous scene where Streep's neck is twisted, her skin and body movements were changed by manipulating pixels on screen. Streep wore a blue screen mask while a computer duplicated and stretched her neck 180 degrees.

Jim Carrey wearing a prosthetic mask and make-up poses for the camera

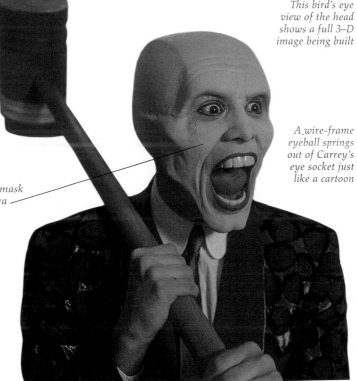

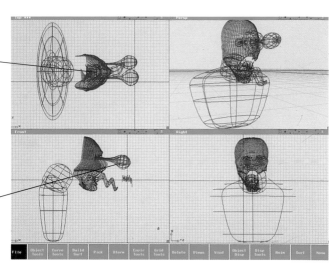

This bird's eye view of the head shows a full 3–D image being built

A wire-frame eyeball springs out of Carrey's eye socket just like a cartoon

1 IN THE BEGINNING...
In the film *The Mask* (1994), bank clerk Stanley Ipkiss (Jim Carrey) dons a mysterious mask and becomes transformed from a bumbling loser into a hilarious super-hero. To bring this colourful cartoon creation to life, special effects experts had to combine live footage of Carrey with state-of-the-art computer generated effects.

2 COMPUTER INPUT
When two-dimensional pencil drawings of the cartoon mask had been assembled, computer experts began building a wire-frame of the mask on screen. A replica image of Jim Carrey's face was manipulated by computer graphics to enable the actor's tongue to spring out of his mouth, and his eyes to shoot out of their sockets! The computer also constructed an entire 3–D frame of the actor's head so that it would look as realistic as possible.

STEVEN SPIELBERG
A visionary of the cinema, director/producer Steven Spielberg has been responsible for some of the biggest film hits of all time. He first burst into the film world with *Jaws* (1975) and followed up with his poetic sci-fi masterpiece *Close Encounters of the Third Kind* (1977). Since then he has created *E.T.* (1982), the Indiana Jones films, and the incredible dinosaurs of *Jurassic Park* (1993) and *The Lost World* (1997). He owns his own film studio, Dreamworks SKG.

"Steven is a genius. I've worked with the best directors in the world, but have never met anybody who has been able to use the language of film as well as him."
GEORGE LUCAS

LIVE ACTION SEQUENCE COMBINED WITH DIGITAL DINOSAUR

1
The awesome T-rex attack in *Jurassic Park* is one of the greatest action sequences in modern cinema. The computer generated dinosaur was first assembled as a wire-frame skeleton and then programmed to interact with a digitally created jeep.

COMPUTER GENERATED TYRANNOSAURUS REX

2
Once the wire-frame monster was fully programmed, digital effects experts combined the digital image with live footage of the actors in the park during a thunderstorm. The clever 3-D wire-frame model was blended with the footage frame by frame.

FINISHED SEQUENCE AS SEEN ON THE SCREEN

3
The dinosaur was fleshed out with computerized bone structure and muscles. Then a special software was used to add the realistic skin textures. The character played by Jeff Goldblum gets more dinosaur than he bargained for!

AN INVISIBLE WORLD

For the film *Ghost* (1990), director Jerry Zucker wanted the ghost of Patrick Swayze to blend in seamlessly with the solid objects he was passing through. To achieve this sequence (left), effects technicians used animation devices in a special computer software package. A "cut-off matte" makes the door cut off the ghost's arm as it passes through, and an "absorption matte" softens the edges of the actor's body as it disappears through the doorway.

THE GHOSTLY IMAGE OF THE HAND PROTRUDING FROM THE DOORWAY MAKES THE ARM LOOK AS IF IT IS EMERGING FROM A THICK LIQUID

PATRICK SWAYZE'S ARM IS BLENDED FRAME BY FRAME WITH THE DOOR THAT IT IS APPARENTLY PASSING THROUGH

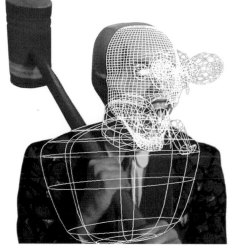

The mallet was one of the elements that was not altered digitally

The eyeballs are exaggerated in true cartoon style

The threatening tongue has been treated digitally too

3 JOINING THE DOTS

The wire-frame Mask image was then combined with the live action footage of Jim Carrey. A computer tracked each movement of the actor and matched the 3–D wire-frame mask to him frame by frame, so that they moved in perfect harmony.

Computer fleshed out image with definition and colour

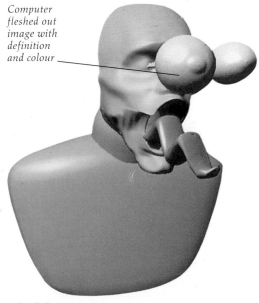

4 MOULDING

When the actor and wire-frame were matched, a special computer fine tuned the digital effects after separating them from any background footage.

5 PUTTING IT ALL TOGETHER

The fantastic combination of digital effects and live action footage has produced this eye-poppin' vision of Jim Carrey under the spell of an ancient mask. *The Mask* was the first film to prove that computer generated effects could produce realistically the distortions of a human body that were already commonplace in cartoon animation.

MORPHING

In the late 1980s and early 1990s, computerized special effects broke into realms that until then had only existed in the imagination, producing some of the most awe-inspiring images of modern cinema. This technological revolution first became apparent in *Willow* (1988), the first film in history to use the technique known as "morphing". This technique allows different images to blend seamlessly or "morph" into each other. To do this the special effects technicians combined blue screen techniques, computer scanning, and specialist digital software. Films such as *The Abyss* (1989), *Terminator 2* (1991), and *Dragonheart* (1997) have all used morphing with spectacular success, pushing cinema into the 21st century.

CGi blends the full headdress with the actor's image

The actor's face takes on the rigid look of the mask

OUT OF THIS WORLD

When actor Jaye Davidson slowly changes into an ancient Egyptian pharaoh on a futuristic planet in *Stargate* (1994), computer-generated morphing was required to show the gradual change from human being to statue. Director Roland Emmerich assembled a special effects team to effect the morph, filming the actor in costume so that this footage could then be blended by computer with film taken of the Egyptian mask.

JEAN-CLAUDE VAN DAMME
IN *TIMECOP* (1996)

CONTACT

In *The Abyss*, an alien sea water pseudopod makes contact with a crew of deep sea divers to create the greatest morphing image in cinema history. Director James Cameron and a crack team of SFX experts used computer graphics to construct a living 3-D saltwater snake, which rippled like real water and reflected the crew's faces. Each actor was laser scanned, and the data fed into a scanner to produce the facial features on the computerized pseudopod.

The blend of face and ancient mask is complete

The liquid metal T-1000 strides out of the fire, slowly changing into a human

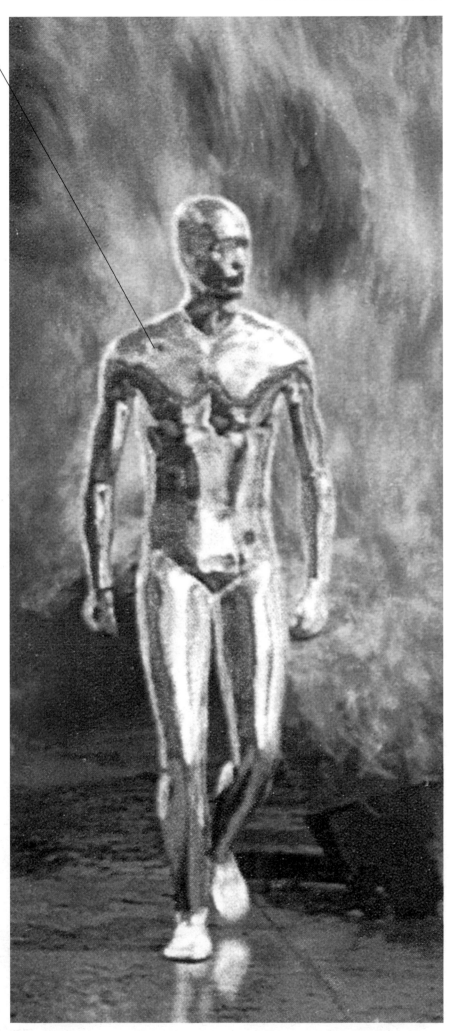

TRAVELLING THROUGH TIME

In the film *Timecop* (1996), actor Jean Claude van Damme is transported to different times in history and different dimensions to bring a ruthless killer to justice. For the scenes involving time travel, special computer effects were used which "morphed" the actor, distorting his physical appearance and making him vanish into thin air.

SILVER DREAM MACHINE

When a deadly T-1000 cyborg has to return from the future to wreak destruction on the present day in *Terminator 2* (1991), the special effects team pushed the boundaries of cinema even further by morphing a chrome robot into a real person while he was walking out of a blazing fire. The shape-shifting liquid cyborg was digitally created as a silver skeleton by computer, and then composited with film of the actor frame by frame. These ground-breaking effects helped win *Terminator 2* the Oscar for best visual effects.

MOTION CAPTURE

Computerized special effects are always looking for new ways to capture human movement. Motion capture is the process of recording an actor's movements using reflective body markers and special high-speed cameras. The cameras' reading of the movement of the body markers is transferred to a computer where they can be built first into a stick person, then into a skeleton, before being built into whatever imaginative virtual character is needed. Motion capture is now widely used in advertising, animation films, music videos, and state-of-the-art video games.

Retro-reflective markers glow red for the camera

REFLECTIVE MARKERS

For the motion capture system to work, the actor must be fitted with lightweight reflective markers on key parts of the body. The movement of the markers is captured by special cameras that combine camera action with the emission of visible red strobes to illuminate and freeze the action.

CAMERA UNIT

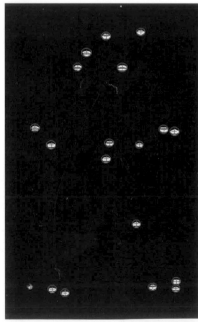

TAKING THE PICTURE
To create an animated character, a basketball-player is fitted with reflective markers on pivotal parts of the body, such as the head, shoulders arms, hips, knees, ankles, and toes.

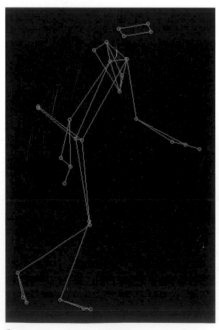

JOINING THE DOTS
Seven cameras then capture the movements of the player. These are fed straight into a computer, where special software designs a basic human frame, joining the marker dots together.

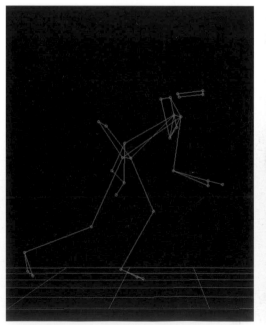

3–D DIGITAL SKELETON
The motion capture software has the ability to transform live 2–D film footage into a digital 3–D version on screen in a matter of seconds. Both player and director can view the movements and suggest changes if needed.

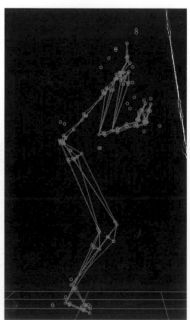

FLESHING OUT
When the body movements have been agreed and edited on screen, the digital skeleton can be "fleshed out", the beginning of the process that will build a new character.

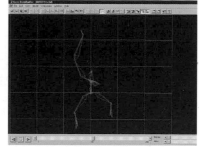

Even the ball has strips of reflective material so that its movements will be recognized

RECORDING SPACE

The area around which the player will move must be calibrated by sweeping the area with a wand on which there are two markers. This defines the area for the computer and gives an exact position for each of the seven cameras used.

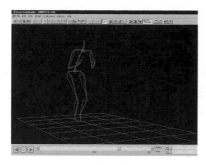

3-D COMPUTER MAGIC

The computer captures data from each of the seven cameras and records every movement of the player. When the data is captured, the information can be manipulated or viewed from different perspectives – for example, from in front (above) or from a bird's-eye point of view (above right).

Markers are placed on special wristbands to capture the complex movements of the forearms

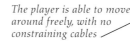

The player is able to move around freely, with no constraining cables

Markers are coated in high quality retro-reflective material that reflects light back

BODY BUILDING

The motion capture skeleton will now move and jump on screen, but it has not yet acquired its new identity. Further software is used to model the new animated character, which will now have built into its structure the fluid movements of a real human being. With motion capture, any kind of movement can be captured, from a running fox to a jumping frog.

FLYING HIGH

Motion capture technology can record the movements of a person, no matter how active they may be. As this player springs into the air with the basketball, the cameras are capturing her movements at 60 frames per second. When the data from the markers is fed into the computer, it can be slowed down, or even edited into completely new movements.

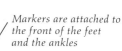

Markers are attached to the front of the feet and the ankles

WHAT NEXT?

Modern special effects are now producing the most incredible images seen in cinema. But what will come next depends on the fertile imagination of SFX experts. Computer-generated actors, shape-shifting monsters, and fantastical visions of outer space could all become screen reality in the near future. The latest movie technology is also developing interactive cinemas, where the audience are moved about in hydraulic seats while watching amazing 3–D movies. Such audience participation, mixed with giant or multi-screen images may all become the cinema of the future. Special effects is also taking giant leaps into the unknown. New techniques such as motion capture (pp. 60–61) may make it possible to show dead screen icons such as Marilyn Monroe or James Dean in new films.

MARILYN MONROE

At Futuroscope the audience sits in hydraulic seats which move them around during the film

Interactive arm pads allow the audience to participate in the movie

Darth Vader battles Luke Skywalker with the help of effects animation in The Empire Strikes Back (1980)

USING THE FORCE

Special effects experts are continually striving to improve and develop their techniques. In the *Star Wars* trilogy different methods were used to produce the stunning lightsabre effect used by Darth Vader and Luke Skywalker. Actors used stick swords wrapped in reflective material for *Star Wars* (1977) which were then manipulated with effects animation. *The Empire Strikes Back* (1980) and *Return of the Jedi* (1983) relied on pure effects animation, while the three new prequels will use state-of-the-art CGi lightsabre effects.

Monroe's legendary legs could soon be walking back onto the screen courtesy of CGi effects

MONROE RETURNS!

Although Hollywood legends James Dean and Humphrey Bogart died years ago, advances in special effects technology could soon see them back on the silver screen. Using a combination of digital trickery and motion camera photography, computer-generated movements could soon recreate the immortal Marilyn Monroe, seen here in *How To Marry A Millionaire* (1953), casting her with modern-day stars.

JOHN DYKSTRA

One of the most important figures in the development of special visual effects, John Dykstra has been an inspiration to many filmmakers. Trained as a special effects cameraman and industrial designer, Dykstra first came to public attention as an inventor of theme park attractions and experimental 3-D filmmaking effects. He achieved huge success with his stunning concepts for the science fiction movies *Silent Running* (1971) and *Star Wars* (1977). As the head of George Lucas' FX company, Industrial Light and Magic, Dykstra orchestrated both the design and photography of all the models and miniatures used in *Star Wars* and received an Oscar for Best Visual Effects. Dykstra also invented the Dykstraflex motion control camera and owns his own company, Apogee, which developed the lavish television series *Battlestar Galactica* (1978–1980).

The Dykstaflex system was built before the advent of personal computers. The system could record moves that could be duplicated whenever needed

Dykstra developed his talents under SFX expert Douglas Trumball on the set of the film 2001: A Space Odyssey

FUTURE FANTASTIC

Special effects are not the only recent advance in movie technology. Movie makers are also developing futuristic cinemas which will make the audience feel as if they are actually participating in the film. At Futuroscope in France, some cinemas have hydraulic seats, interactive arm pads, and 180 degree screens to create the ultimate movie experience. Modern 3–D headwear has also been developed to bring films to life.

Flames are added digitally to 3–D animated beast

Tron used futuristic animation effects to conjure these speedbikes

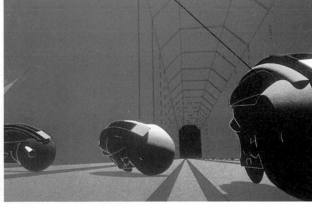

COMPUTER MOVIE

Hollywood has been toying with the idea of fully computerized films for over a decade. Disney's *Tron* (1982) shows Jeff Bridges being sucked into a powerful computer where he must try and survive a deadly videogame. Groundbreaking effects, which cost millions of dollars, included animated speedbikes and illuminated body costumes. Although the film failed at the box-office, it pushed the boundaries of special effects into a new realm.

COMPUTER FUTURE

Many future movies will be created or enhanced on screen, using computer generated imagery (CGi). This 3–D animated dragon has been created as a wire frame image (pp. 54–55), before being fleshed out, enhanced and lit carefully – all on a computer. The animated film *Toy Story* (1996) is perhaps the clearest example of the future of special effects in the cinema. It was the first full-length CGi animated film, using more than one hundred high-powered computers to develop the 3–D adventures of Buzz Lightyear and Woody. The amazing colour, texture, lighting, and detail of computerized animation in films like this will stretch the limits of digital technology.

Index

Acknowledgements

Additional photography Steve Gorton, Frank Greenaway, Gary Ombler, Alex Wilson
Design and editorial assistance Goldberry Broad, Diane Clouting, Jill Plank, Nicky Roberts, Maggie Tingle
Models Emma Bowden, Tom Buddle, Iain Morris, Kati Poynor, Tim Scott, Lucy Smith, Andy Warner
Dorling Kindersley would also like to thank Jean-Jacques Annaud and Mandalay Entertainment for permission to photograph the matte painting from *Seven Years in Tibet*, 1997 (p. 17); Channel Four Equinox/The Mission Film & Television, Joanne Ray, and Geraldine Quinn for permission to photograph the miniature set (pp. 28–31); George Cottle; Simon Crane; Lindy Diamond; Ben Dray; Doug Ferris; Stuart Frossell; Aron Green; Nick Harrison of Weird and Wonderful; Niki Lyons, Jamie Courtier, Adrienne Gardner, and Dan Bateman of Jim Henson's Creature Shop; James Mckeown; Rick Mietkowski; Dave Morgan; Ian Morse; Steve North; Dave Pearson; Will Petty; Stuart Ray; Chris Reynolds of BBC Special Effects; Mike Uden and Paul Hannaford of Rushes; Gordon Seagrove; Robert Shacklady; Leigh Took and Ben Hall; Françoise Valentine; Kate Wyhowska of Polygram
Index Hilary Bird
Jacket design Mark Haygarth

The publisher would like to thank the following for their kind permission to reproduce their photographs
a=above; b=below; c=centre; l=left; r=right; t=top; BFI=The British Film Institute, JFC=The Joel Finler Collection, RGA=The Ronald Grant Archive
The Abyss, 1989, 20th Century Fox, 58bl, (courtesy Corbis/Everett); *The Adventures of Pinocchio*, © 1996, New Line Productions, Inc. All rights reserved. Photos appear courtesy of New Line Productions, Inc. and Industrial Light & Magic, 23tl, 23r, 23c, 23bl; *Alien*, 1979, 20th Century Fox, 34tr, (courtesy RGA); *Batman*, 1989, Warner Bros., 16tr, 16cr, 16bl, 16br; *Black Narcissus*, 1946, GFD/The Archers, 17tc, 17tr, 17tra, (courtesy JFC); *Blown Away*, 1992, MGM/ Trilogy, 44cl, (courtesy Moviestore); *The Borrowers*, 1997, Polygram, 8bc, 8br, 26tr, 26c, 27; *A Bridge Too Far*, United Artists/ Joseph E. Levine, 40br, (courtesy Kobal); 47, (courtesy BFI); *Buddy*, 1997, Jim Henson's Creature Shop, 24–5, 24 bl, 25tr, 25 cr, 25br; *Clash of the Titans*, 1981, MGM, 22tr, (courtesy RGA); *Cliffhanger*, 1993, Tri-star, 11bl, 38bl, 52tr, (courtesy Kobal); *Con Air*, 1997, Touchstone/Buena Vista/ Bruckheimer, 18cl, (courtesy Moviestore); *Die Hard 2*, 1990, 20th Century Fox, 49tl, (courtesy RGA); 44tl, (courtesy Moviestore); *Doctor Zhivago*, 1965, MGM/ David Lean/Carlo Ponti, 48c, (courtesy Kobal); *The Empire Strikes Back™*, © Lucasfilm Ltd 1980, 14bl; *Fantastic Voyage*, 1966, 20th Century Fox, 26cl, (courtesy Kobal); *The Fifth Element*, 1997, Columbia/ Gaumont, 17tl, (courtesy Moviestore); *Gentlemen Prefer Blondes*, 1947, 20th Century Fox, 62l, (courtesy Kobal); *Ghost*, 1990, UIP/ Paramount/Howard W. Koch, 57tc, 57tl, (courtesy BFI); *Ghostbusters*, 1984, Columbia/ Delphi, 51bl; *Glory*, 1989, Columbia Tri-Star, 46bc, (courtesy Moviestore); *Godzilla*, Toho Productions, 22tl; *Goldeneye*, 1995, UIP/UA/ EON/DANJAQ, 41tr, (courtesy Moviestore); *Gone with the Wind*, 1939, MGM/Selznick, 9tc, 10crb, (courtesy JFC); *Grand Prix*, 1966, MGM/

Douglas & Lewis, 10cr, (courtesy JFC); *Gullivers Travels*, 26bl, Jim Henson's Creature Shop, (courtesy Channel 4); *Hard Rain*, 1998, Polygram, 13tr, 50bl; *Honey I Shrunk the Kids*, 1989, Warner Bros./The Walt Disney Co./Doric, 39br; *Independence Day*, 1996, 20th Century Fox, 6–7tc, (courtesy RGA); 21tr, 31cr, 31br; *Jason and the Argonauts*, 1963, Columbia/James H. Schneer, 14c, (courtesy Kobal); *The Last Action Hero*, 1993, Columbia, 46tl, (courtesy Kobal); *Lethal Weapon*, 1987, Warner Bros., 40c, 40crb, 41bl, 41br, (courtesy RGA); *Little Big Man*, 1970, Stockbridge/Hiller/Cinema Centre, 33tl, (courtesy JFC); *Lost in Space*, 1998, New Line Cinema/Space Dog Productions 18–19; *Mary Poppins*, 1964, The Walt Disney Co., 15bl, (courtesy JFC); *The Mask*, © 1994, New Line Productions, Inc. All rights reserved. Photos appear courtesy of New Line Productions, Inc. and Industrial Light & Magic, 56c, 56cr,57cl, 57cr, 57bl; *Memoirs of an Invisible Man*, 1992, Warner Bros., 19tl, 19tr; *Mission Impossible*, 1996, Paramount, 7cl, 39tr; *The Mosquito Coast*, 1986, Paramount, 51b, 51cr, (courtesy RGA); *Oliver!* 1968, Columbia/ Warwick/ Romulus, 48bl, (courtesy Pictorial Press); *Raiders of the Lost Ark*, 1981, Paramount/Lucasfilm, 31tc, (courtesy BFI); *Return of the Jedi™*, © R. Mcgrath/Lucasfilm Ltd 1983, 20cra; *The Rock*, 1996, Hollywood Pictures, 10cl, (courtesy Moviestore); *Rumble in the Bronx*, 1995, Golden Harvest/Maple Ridge Films/New Line Cinema, 10bc; *Speed 2 – Cruise Control*, 1997, 20th Century Fox/Blue Tulip, 40bc, (courtesy Moviestore); *The Spy Who Loved Me*, 1977, UA/EON, 52cl, (courtesy Moviestore); *Star Wars™*, © Lucasfilm Ltd 1977, 20t, 62c; *Stargate*, 1994, Guild/Canal/Centropolis/Carolco, 58–59t; *Superman*, 1978, Warner Bros., 15cr; *Terminator 2: Judgement Day*, 1991, Guild, 59r, (courtesy RGA); *Three Coins in the

Fountain*, 1954, 20th Century Fox, 15tl, (courtesy JFC); *Timecop*, 1994, Largo/JVC/ Signature/Renaissance/Dark Horse, 58br, 59bl, (courtesy RGA); *Tron*, 1982, The Walt Disney Co., 63bl, (courtesy RGA); *True Lies*, 1994, 20th Century Fox/Lightstorm, 46bl, (courtesy BFI); *2001: A Space Odyssey*, 1968, MGM/Stanley Kubrick, 20cr, 20bc, (courtesy JFC); 20br, (courtesy BFI); *Volcano*, 1997, 20th Century Fox, 50cr; *Voyage to the Moon*, 1902, 14tr, (courtesy RGA); *The Wild Bunch*, 1969, Warner Seven Arts, 32cla, (courtesy JFC); *The Wizard of Oz*, 1939, MGM, 9b, (courtesy Museum of the Moving Image); 16cl (courtesy RGA); *You Only Live Twice*, 1967, UA/EON, 18tr (courtesy RGA); The Ronald Grant Archive: 32tr; Moviestore: 11br; Oxberry: 15br; Rex Features: 20bl, 62bc.

Copyright by Universal City Studios, Inc., courtesy of Universal Studios Publishing Rights. All rights reserved: *Backdraft*, 1991, jacket back flap b, 13tl, (courtesy Moviestore); 42cl, (courtesy RGA); *The Dark Crystal*, 1982, 8bl; *Death Becomes Her*, 1992, jacket front tc (courtesy Moviestore), 56tl, (courtesy Moviestore); *Dragonheart*, 1996, 54cl; *E.T. The Extra-Terrestrial*, 1982, 8tr, (courtesy Kobal), 28tl; *The Hunchback of Notre Dame*, 1923, 32cra, (courtesy Moviestore); *The Incredible Shrinking Man*, 1957, 26tl, (courtesy Moviestore); *Jurassic Park*, 1993, 56bca, 56bc, 56bl, 56br.

Jacket *Buddy*, 1997, Jim Henson's Creature Shop, front l, back tl; *The Mask*, © 1994, New Line Productions, Inc. All rights reserved. Courtesy of New Line Productions, Inc. and Industrial Light & Magic, front br; Gorton and Painter front tcl, tcr, back br; Mike Valentine back tr.